IMAGES
of America

PITTSBURGH'S
GOLDEN AGE OF RADIO

KQV's Jeff Christie served as honorary chairman of the Variety Club's Celebrity Hike for Handicapped Children walkathon in 1973. He joined KQV from WIXZ, where he hosted mornings as Bachelor Jeff. After working in Kansas City, he returned to KQV for a brief period in 1975. Today he is better known under his real name, Rush Limbaugh. (Author's collection.)

ON THE COVER: KDKA was the first radio station to offer uninterrupted commercially licensed service with the broadcast of the Harding-Cox elections on November 20, 1920, anchored by Leo Rosenberg. Previously stations only broadcast experimentally or for a few hours at a time on an irregular basis. The broadcast originated from a shack on the roof of a Westinghouse Electric Company building in East Pittsburgh. (Courtesy KDKA.)

IMAGES
of America

PITTSBURGH'S
GOLDEN AGE OF RADIO

Ed Salamon

ARCADIA
PUBLISHING

Published by Arcadia Publishing
Charleston SC, Chicago IL, Portsmouth NH, San Francisco CA

Printed in the United States of America

Library of Congress Control Number: 2009930883

For all general information contact Arcadia Publishing at:
Telephone 843-853-2070
Fax 843-853-0044
E-mail sales@arcadiapublishing.com
For customer service and orders:
Toll-Free 1-888-313-2665

Visit us on the Internet at www.arcadiapublishing.com

*Dedicated to my colleagues in Pittsburgh radio and to
all of those readers who listened to our stations.*

CONTENTS

Acknowledgments   6

Introduction   7

1.   Commercial Radio Begins   11

2.   AM Radio Reinvents Itself   41

3.   The Growth of FM Radio   87

ACKNOWLEDGMENTS

Thanks to all those who helped with information and/or photographs: Marshall Adams, Timothy G. Adams, Anthony Alfonsi, Dex Allen, Ira Apple, Buzzy Beck, Bobby Bennett, Judy Hinds Boehm, Jack Bogut, Don Bombard, Ronald "Buzz" Brindle, Chuck Brinkman, Jay Brooks, Terry Caywood, Porky Chedwick, Lou Christie, Rich Cline, Bob DeCarlo, Dwight Douglas, Chuck Dunaway, Carl Eckels, Frank Gottlieb, Bob Harper, Bill Hinds, Batt Johnson, John Long, Perry Marshall, Robin Marshall, Warren Maurer, Mike McGann, Cindy Mozingo, Joe Negri, Denise Oliver, Jim Riggs, Jimmy Roach, Mark Roberts, John Rook, Jimmie Ross, Jeff Roteman, Drew Salamon, Jessie Scott, Ed Sherlock, Chris Shovlin, Diane Sutter, John Taylor, Mike Thompson, Murray Tucker, Bobby Vinton, Ed Weigle, Rob Wesley, and Bob Wood.

Thanks to my wife, Katy Salamon, for proofreading and editing. Thanks to Kristen England for photograph editing and restoration.

All images not specifically credited are from the author's collection.

INTRODUCTION

Some of my earliest memories are listening to the big console radio in the living room—radio dramas (*The Lone Ranger* was my favorite), live music programs, and, of course, the deejay shows. One of my favorite stations was WHOD mostly because it was the easiest for me as a child to find, since it was the first station on our radio's dial with good reception. I experienced the birth of rock and roll and the popularity of rhythm and blues through radio. The radio became a constant companion when I received an early transistor radio as a birthday present. I was fortunate to work in radio, and I got to know as friends many of the people I had listened to on the radio. I am glad to have the opportunity to write this book because it preserves history that is important to a lot of Pittsburghers. The reader should appreciate that memories of those involved, as well as written sources, may differ. With the changes in format and ownership over the years, very few radio stations saved much of their history. Radio personalities are a mobile group, and whatever they might save from their stations often disappears in their moves. Appreciating the scarcity of these images, I am particularly grateful to the contributors who have saved photographs and promotional pieces and are sharing them in this book.

The Federal Communications Commission recognizes that commercial radio began in Pittsburgh at KDKA on November 2, 1920, because KDKA was granted the first commercial license, after which it broadcast on a regular schedule. That first broadcast, the Harding-Cox election, was anchored by Leo Rosenberg. Since radio broadcasting originated largely with inventors and hobbyists transmitting on an irregular basis, many other entities have claimed to originating radio. Most historians agree that radio was an outgrowth of telegraphy. In 1865, Dr. Mahlon Loomis of Washington, D.C., began tinkering with the idea of wireless messaging. In 1887, Heinrich Hertz detected and produced the first radio waves. Hertz was actually studying a fellow scientist's data when he accidently set up a spark transmitter and receiver. In 1892, Nathan D. Stubblefield of Murray, Kentucky, demonstrated wireless voice and music broadcasts. In 1893, Nikola Tesla demonstrated wireless broadcasts in St. Louis. In 1895, Guglielmo Marconi began wireless demonstrations in Italy. In 1906, Reginald Fessenden talked, sang, and played violin into a wireless telephone that he invented at Brant Rock, Massachusetts. In 1907, Lee Deforest broadcast the first ship-to-shore message from the steam yacht *Thelma* and broadcast phonograph records from the navy fleet. Disliking the name "wireless," he called his broadcasts "radio." *Radio*, in the sense of wireless transmission, had first been used as a prefix by the French physicist Eduard Branley in 1897, based on the verb *radiate*. *Radio* as a noun is credited to Waldo Warren, an advertising man. Some have argued that station WWJ in Detroit, owned by the *Detroit News*, was the first radio station. It began regular broadcasts on August 20, 1920, using the call sign 8MK, an amateur license. In Pittsburgh, Frank Conrad operated KDKA's predecessor, 75-watt 8XK from Wilkinsburg, beginning in 1916. Conrad first became interested in radio in 1912. In order to settle a $5 bet with a coworker on the accuracy of his $12 watch, Conrad built a small receiver to hear time signals from the Naval Observatory in Arlington, Virginia. Conrad won the bet. In November 1919, KQV signed on as 8ZAE with an amateur license.

The primary purpose of KDKA was to encourage the sale of radio receivers. At this time, Westinghouse and other manufacturers began to build self-contained radio sets that any consumer could use. Before this time, those who wanted to hear radio would have to build their own crystal sets. Radio was replacing the piano as the primary source of in-home entertainment, since listeners in various locations could now enjoy the same experience. KDKA's success inspired an explosion of radio stations. By 1921, Westinghouse had founded three additional stations: WJZ in Newark, KYW in Chicago, and WBZ in Springfield, Massachusetts. That same year, Harold W. Arlen was the first person ever hired as a full-time radio announcer and Frank Mullen became the first farm broadcaster. A number of other important radio events occurred in Pittsburgh in 1921. On January 2, KDKA aired the first regularly scheduled church service broadcast from Calvary Episcopal Church in Pittsburgh. On January 19, experimental station 8ZAE began using the call letters KQV (King of the Quaker Valley), although it did not receive its commercial license until the following year. For a time, the station was used to broadcast on demand to demonstrate radios at owner Doubleday-Hill Electric Company's store downtown. On May 3, WCAE, owned by Kaufmann and Baer Department Store, signed on. On August 5, Harold Arlen became the first person to broadcast a Major League Baseball game, using a converted telephone as a microphone. That same year, T. J. Vastine conducted the first band concert ever broadcast on radio at KDKA. On November 21, KDKA instituted the first children's programming with regular broadcasts of bedtime stories. When WJAS, owned by Pittsburgh Radio Supply House, Inc., signed on December 12, 1922, Pittsburgh had four commercial radio stations.

In 1923, the AM band as we know it was established. The Commerce Department, under whom radio regulation fell at the time, needed to prevent signal interference as more stations applied for commercial licenses. The official basis for designating these settings was changed from wavelengths to frequencies, expressed in kilocycles (today known as kilohertz, or kHz). Eighty-one frequencies were set aside in 10-kHz steps, from 550 kHz to 1350 kHz. That same year, Frank Mullen became the first full-time farm reporter originating his KDKA broadcasts from National Stockman and Farmer in East Liberty. By 1925, there were nearly 600 licensed commercial radio stations in the United States. By 1926, Westinghouse joined with RCA and General Electric to form the first radio network, the National Broadcasting Company, NBC. NBC maintained studios in New York and originated programs, many by vaudevillians, including *The Happiness Boys*, which was carried in Pittsburgh by KDKA. By January 1927, NBC separated its programming into two networks: the Red (WEAF) Network and the Blue (WJZ) Network, identified after their key stations in New York City. In Pittsburgh, WCAE became the Red Network affiliate. KDKA was a Blue Network affiliate until switching to the Red Network in 1941. These national shows were combined with locally produced shows, including KDKA's *Little Symphony Orchestra*, *Westinghouse Band*, and *Dilworth's Little German Band*. In 1927, the Federal Radio Commission was established specifically to regulate radio.

In the 1930s, Joe Negri performed on *Uncle Harold*, *Uncle Sammy*, *Pittsburgh on Parade*, and various other children's shows. KDKA listeners first heard "Uncle Ed" Schaughency on the *Kiddies Club*. Dave Garroway, later host of the NBC *Today Show*, started his career in broadcasting at KDKA. Rosey Rowswell called the Pittsburgh Pirates' games. Dick Powell, then master of ceremonies at the Enright and later Stanley theaters, sang on radio before leaving Pittsburgh to become a movie star. In 1934, the Federal Communication Commission succeeded the Federal Radio Commission as radio's regulator. By the mid-1930s, programs featuring recorded music began to grow in popularity, displacing live programming. The success of *Make Believe Ballroom* hosted by Martin Block on New York's WNEW was influential. In 1936, the first radio ratings phone survey by Crossley, Neilsen, and Hooper would follow.

In 1940, Slim Bryant and the Wild Cats came to Pittsburgh and played on *The Farm Show* on KDKA from then through 1959. In 1941, the North American Radio Broadcast Agreement caused most AM stations to change frequencies and allowed KDKA to broadcast at 50,000 watts full-time with a non-directional signal. The first commercial FM station in Pittsburgh, WWSW's sister station WMOT (now 3WS), also went on the air in 1941. It was followed about a year later by KDKA-FM (now WLTJ). During the years immediately preceding and during World War II, radio was a source of news, inspiration, and patriotic support. Stations sponsored war bond rallies. In 1945, KQV became a Mutual affiliate and broadcast *The Lone Ranger*. Many new radio stations were established after the war. Daytimers WPIT and WPGH and McKeesport radio station WEDO, as well as WMCK and Braddock's WLOA, were all on the air by the end of 1947. WHOD began broadcasting from Homestead in 1948. At that time, the great majority of radio stations were affiliated with one of the four national networks: NBC, CBS (established 1927), ABC (formerly the NBC Blue Network), and the Mutual Broadcasting System (established in 1934).

In the 1950s, the popularity of television forced radio to reinvent itself. Many of television's earliest performers came from radio, creating a talent drain on the radio networks. Gradually stations began to wean themselves from network programming to locally originated disc jockey shows. Radio stations started to choose a consistent style of programming throughout the day, rather than varying from show to show. Rhythm and blues, country, and the new rock and roll grew in popularity. WPGH changed call letters to WILY and its format to rhythm and blues. In 1956, WHOD changed call letters to WAMO and format to full-time country, except for Porky Chedwick, who had begun playing rhythm and blues oldies some years earlier. Barry Kaye (WJAS), Jay Michaels (WCAE), and Al Nobel (KQV) played rock and roll on their programs. In 1957, WJAS was purchased by the NBC Radio Network, who renamed it WAMP (in 1960, it would revert to WJAS). That October, WILY changed call letters to WEEP and their format, becoming Pittsburgh's first full-time Top 40 station. After WILY abandoned rhythm and blues, WAMO adopted that format. On January 13, 1958, KQV became the first network-owned station anywhere to switch to Top 40. WEEP versus KQV was the first of Pittsburgh's Top 40 battles.

In 1961, WCAE became WRYT and played only "good music," such as standards, show tunes, and instrumentals. That same year, the U.S. Congress authorized FM stereo. The Pittsburgh FM dial offered "Beautiful Music" and, for a short while, jazz on WAMO's FM sister station, WAZZ. In 1964, a new rating service, Arbitron, debuted and became the prevailing measure of local radio listening. KDKA competed with KQV for Beatles' fans. Throughout the 1960s, live concerts were a common radio promotion. In the mid-1960s, WZUM challenged WAMO for Pittsburgh's rhythm and blues radio audience. In the battle for the Top 40 audience, WEEP changed its call letters to WYRE and back again to WEEP, before finally switching to a country format in 1966. In February 1969, new owners Westchester Broadcasting Company changed call letter of McKeesport's WMCK to WIXZ and challenged KQV's Top 40 supremacy. The FCC mandated separation of AM and FM effective in 1967. As a result, FM stations could no longer simulcast more than 50 percent of their parent station. Since few listeners had FM receivers, stations could invest little in the programming. Most FM stations carried automated programming. Others became an opportunity for young people willing to work for the low salaries the new medium offered. Coincidentally, rock artists at this time were releasing popular records thought to be too long or otherwise inappropriate for AM radio. This provided the opportunity for the establishment of underground or progressive formats, pioneered in Pittsburgh by Ken Reeth as Brother Love on WAMO-FM and by KQV-FM, as an affiliate of the ABC Radio's FM Network's "Love Format." In 1971, KQV-FM changed call letters to WDVE and evolved into a FM rock format. In the late 1960s, WRYT changed to WTAE and a middle-of-the-road format.

By the 1970s, radio advertisers were becoming more knowledgeable about their customers and stations' target audiences became more defined. Radio stations likewise began to implement consumer research. Leading stations KDKA and KQV, who had courted the teen audience, became more adult in their approach in order to attract a greater share of advertiser dollars. In the mid-1970s, considered WTAE's most successful era, the station changed from middle-of-the-road to an adult contemporary format. Seeing opportunity in a disenfranchised teen audience, 13-Q challenged KQV in one of the last Top 40 battles on AM radio. In 1974, Pittsburgh got its first Top 40 FM station, WPEZ, which competed with 13-Q. Country radio finally flourished at WEEP. There was more spoken word programming on AM in 1975, as KQV switched to all news. By 1977, station 13-Q had new owners, who tried adult contemporary and in 1979 reimaged the station as 1320 WKTQ. In 1978, FM listenership exceeded AM listenership for the first time.

One

COMMERCIAL RADIO
BEGINS

Since Pittsburgh is the birthplace of commercial radio, it was the location of many of the medium's firsts. Radio soon became dependent on network programming. Many of vaudeville's biggest stars, including Will Rogers, Fred Allen, and Eddie Cantor, made the transition to radio. The major network shows generally originated from New York, Chicago, and Los Angeles, but as network affiliates, Pittsburgh stations would sometimes originate national programs.

By the 1940s, radio relied mostly on network and syndicators for its more popular programming, much as television would later. WWSW broadcast *Tales from Our Town*, *The Harry James Orchestra*, and *The Claude Thornhill Orchestra*. WCAE aired *Orphan Annie*, *Jack Armstrong*, *The Lone Ranger*, *Gabriel Heater*, local sports with Rosey Rowswell, and local music with the Baron Elliott Orchestra. WJAS provided *Amos and Andy*, *Kate Smith*, and *The Goldbergs*. KQV's schedule included *John's Other Wife*, *Just Plain Bill*, *Burns and Allen*, *Lum and Abner*, and local sports with Bob Prince. KDKA offered *Ma Perkins*, *Stella Dallas*, and *Lowell Thomas*, as well as local musical performers Slim Bryant and his Wildcats and the Bernie Armstrong Orchestra.

Beginning in 1919, Pittsburgher Frank Conrad broadcast regularly from his garage in Wilkinsburg on 8XK. He presented live music and talk, as well as records provided by the Hamilton Music Store in Wilkinsburg in exchange for promotion (arguably qualifying as the first radio commercial). Conrad supervised the building of the first KDKA studios. He became responsible for the founding of the first licensed broadcast station in the world when KDKA broadcast the results of the Harding-Cox election shortly after receiving its commercial call letters. Conrad was not there to witness the historical broadcast, however. Worried that the station might go down, he was sitting in his garage with his own transmitter as a backup. (Courtesy KDKA.)

KDKA's transmitter room in the early 1920s was the space originally used to broadcast the Harding-Cox election returns. For the first six months of its existence, programs originated either as phonograph records played in a shack atop the Westinghouse plant or from churches, theaters, hotels, or other remote points. In May 1921, it was decided to pitch a tent on the roof next to the transmitter room as a studio. (Courtesy KDKA.)

On January 2, 1921, KDKA aired the first regularly scheduled church service broadcast from Calvary Episcopal Church in Pittsburgh. Religious programming became a mainstay of commercial radio as church leaders found that radio could bring their message to more people than they would be able to reach in person. This 1923 photograph is one of the earliest of a religious radio broadcast. (Courtesy KDKA.)

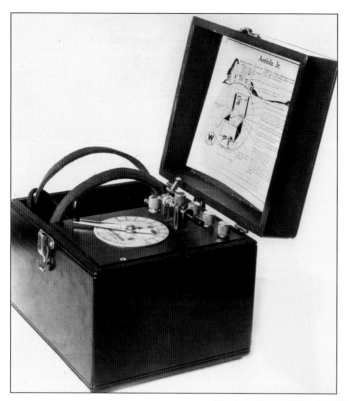

KDKA's regular broadcast schedule was very successful in promoting Westinghouse radio receiver sales to the general public. In 1921, Westinghouse introduced the first popularly priced home radio receiver, the Aeriola Jr. crystal set. In order to better cover the country, Westinghouse also established additional radio stations WJZ, Newark, New Jersey; KWY, Chicago, Illinois; and WBZ, Springfield, Massachusetts. (Courtesy KDKA.)

In 1921, T. J. Vastine conducted the first band concert broadcast on radio over KDKA. Later live music broadcasts—both in studio and from remote locations such as ballrooms—would become a staple of radio programming. This first band concert broadcast was by the Westinghouse band, made up of company employees. (Courtesy KDKA.)

Harold W. Arlin was the first person to be employed as a full-time radio announcer. He also served as the station's first program director. Between recorded or live music, he would read news headlines and community service bulletins. In April 1921, Arlin became one of the first sports announcers when he broadcast a prize fight. On August 5 of that year, he was the first to broadcast a Major League Baseball game. The following month, Arlin was the first to broadcast football, a college game between Pitt and West Virginia. (Courtesy KDKA.)

Another of radio's firsts that originated in Pittsburgh was children's programming. It began with a nightly broadcast of bedtime stories, which was instituted by KDKA on November 19, 1921. These bedtime stories became one of KDKA's most successful programs, led to similar shows at radio stations across the country, and also encouraged broadcasters to develop other programs for children. (Courtesy KDKA.)

Eddie Cantor was heard on KDKA radio as early as February 3, 1922, at which point he was already a successful vaudeville, Broadway, and recording star. Cantor was a natural for the new medium, and in the 1930s, he joined the NBC Network's *Chase and Sanborn Hour*, where he was said to be the world's highest paid radio entertainer. He followed that with his own NBC show, *Time to Smile*. (Courtesy KDKA.)

RADIO
BROADCASTING
ⓦ NEWS ⓦ

Sixty-sixth Week Broadcasting   March 26, 1922   KDKA Edition.   Vol. I.   No.

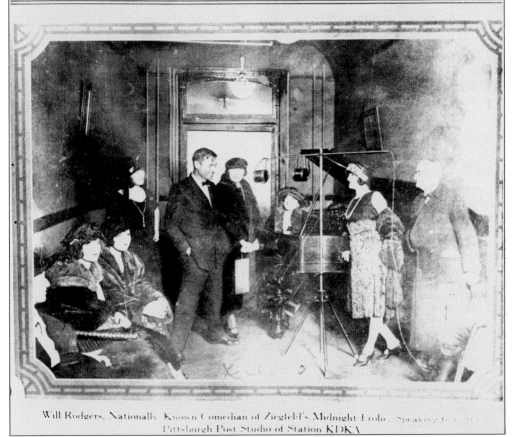

Will Rodgers, Nationally Known Comedian of Ziegfeld's Midnight Frolic, Speaking from the Pittsburgh Post Studio of Station KDKA

The front cover photograph of the March 26, 1922, *Radio Broadcasting News* was captioned, "Will Rodgers [sic], nationally known comedian at Ziegfeld's Midnight Frolic, speaking at the Pittsburgh Post Studio of KDKA." This is considered Rogers's first radio broadcast. By 1935, his weekly Sunday evening show, *The Gulf Headliners*, was ranked among the top 15 radio programs in the country.

The first orchestra developed specifically for broadcast originated at KDKA. Victor Saudek, pictured front and center, conducted KDKA's Little Symphony Orchestra in 1922. In addition to being a noted conductor, Saudek was an accomplished flautist. He also taught the flute and later served on the music faculty of the Carnegie Institute of Technology. (Courtesy KDKA.)

This is KDKA radio's downtown studios in the William Penn Hotel at Christmas 1922. Draperies served acoustic as well as decorative purposes. KDKA also had a studio in the Westinghouse building in East Pittsburgh. These were big improvements over KDKA's former studio, which was a tent on the roof next to the transmitter room. Early radio listeners came to expect the whistle of a passing freight train nightly at 8:30. (Courtesy KDKA.)

In 1920, KDKA was the first station to offer daily farm reports. Frank Mullen became the first full-time farm broadcaster. He hosted KDKA's pioneer farm program from a studio located at the publication *National Stockman and Farmer*, in East Liberty, beginning in 1923. Mullen later became director of information at RCA and later vice president and general manager of NBC, where he was instrumental in the introduction of television. (Courtesy KDKA.)

This 1926 photograph shows a KDKA car and crew with remote equipment in front of the Syria Mosque, a performance hall in Oakland that was home to many live events and one of KDKA's origination, or pick-up, points. In the 1940s, WCAE would originate a Mutual Broadcasting Network program with the Pittsburgh Symphony from the Syria Mosque. (Courtesy KDKA.)

In 1926, Westinghouse joined with RCA and General Electric to form the first permanent radio network, the National Broadcasting Company, NBC. *The Happiness Boys* (Billy Jones and Ernie Hare) was one of the first network programs broadcast. When NBC split into the Red and Blue Networks, KDKA became Pittsburgh's Blue Network affiliate until 1941, when it switched to the Red Network. (Courtesy KDKA.)

In the 1926–1927 season, the NBC Red Network carried the *Cliquot Club Eskimos*. They were a jazz group that became one of the biggest radio stars of the 1930s. WCAE was the Red Network affiliate in Pittsburgh at the time, so it likely carried this show. The Red Network also offered the *Major Bowes Family* and the *A&P Gypsies*. (Courtesy KDKA.)

Featured Every Thursday Evening at 6:30 over KDKA

Dilworth's Little German Band appeared on KDKA radio in the late 1920s and early 1930s. They were led by conductor Gus Smaltz and featured Schnitzel, their dog mascot. Here they are pictured in front of KDKA microphones with the station's chief announcer, Louie Kaufman. (Courtesy KDKA.)

In the early 1930s, Dick Powell, master of ceremonies at the Enright and later Stanley theaters, sang on local radio before leaving Pittsburgh to become a movie star. He continued to appear in both singing and dramatic roles on network radio shows into the 1950s, including *The Old Gold Program* (CBS), *Lux Radio Theater* (CBS), *Maxwell House Coffee Time* (NBC), and his own *Dick Powell Program* for NBC.

Bill Hinds (left) was an announcer on WCAE before moving to KDKA in 1933. There he was teamed with Buzz Aston (right) as *Buzz and Bill*. After World War II, the duo returned to Pittsburgh radio on WJAS. By the mid-1950s, Hinds was hosting the morning radio show on WJAS in addition to appearing on the *Buzz and Bill* television show. From 1958 to 1970, he hosted a show on WWSW. (Courtesy Judith Hinds Boehm.)

As a child performer, Joe Negri performed on various stations, learning a new song every week. He also appeared in theatrical and stage productions throughout the tristate area. He was chosen as one of Pittsburgh's Stars of Tomorrow. Negri took up the ukulele so that he could accompany himself. He quit performing when his voice changed. (Courtesy Joe Negri.)

Dirigibles were popular in the 1930s, and according to KDKA, this is a photograph of a test of an experimental antenna during that time period in the Pittsburgh area. The Westinghouse Electric Company had been a pioneer in radio broadcasting and continued to refine radio transmission technology during the medium's early years. (Courtesy KDKA.)

In 1938, the KDKA Orchestra was conducted by Maurice Spitalny. Spitalny is famous for another Pittsburgh first. Around 1934, Spitalny explained to his waiter at the William Penn Hotel how he wanted his salad prepared: julienned ham, turkey breast, and Swiss cheese on a bed of greens, tomatoes, and hard-cooked eggs, with a mayonnaise dressing. The word spread, and soon other restaurants were offering their version of the Maurice Salad. (Courtesy KDKA.)

Dave Garroway's first broadcasting job was as a KDKA staff announcer from 1938 to 1940. He was a former NBC radio page and fresh from NBC's school for announcers, reportedly graduating 23 in a class of 24. His reports from a hot-air balloon, from a U.S. Navy submarine in the Ohio River, and from deep inside a coal mine earned Garroway (above right) a reputation for finding a good story in unusual places. He left KDKA to enlist in the navy for World War II. He is best remembered as founding host of NBC TV's *Today Show*. (Courtesy KDKA.)

Albert Kennedy "Rosey" Rowswell was hired as the Pirates' first full-time announcer in 1936 and one of the first broadcasters to root for their team. He developed a colorful vocabulary: the team was "the Buccos," a Pirates extra base hit was a "doozie marooney," a strikeout was a "dipsy-doodle," and the bases were never "loaded," they were "FOB" (full of Bucs). When Rowswell died after the 1954 season, Bob Prince took over the play-by-play duties. At the time of his death, Rowswell was said to be the Major League announcer with the most years of consecutive service to a team. (Courtesy Joe Tucker Archives/Murray Tucker.)

Pittsburgh Pirates announcer Rosey Rowswell is shown riding with Aunt Minnie. Whenever there was an out-of-the-park home run, Rowswell would say, "Raise the window, Aunt Minnie, here it comes," followed by the sound effect of breaking glass, to which Rowswell responded, "Aunt Minnie never made it." According to KDKA, this photograph promoted a television demonstration in the 1930s. In 1955, the Pirates broadcasts moved from WJAS to KDKA. (Courtesy KDKA.)

Buzz Aston (left) performed on WWSW before moving to KDKA, where he emceed the variety show *Memory Time* in the 1930s. He teamed with announcer Bill Hinds (right) for a music and comedy program, *The Buzz and Bill Show*. In 1950, Buzz and Bill started a seven-year run on WDTV television, which later became KDKA-TV, located in the Chamber of Commerce Building where they were working at WJAS. (Courtesy Judith Hinds Boehm.)

KDKA *War Bond Wagon* shows were presented in many communities within the station's coverage area during World War II. These live variety shows helped to raise money for the U.S. Treasury Department by encouraging the audience to buy war bonds. Direct sale of war bonds reached over $1 million, and KDKA participated in other rallies and promotions that resulted in the sale of $6.6 million in bonds. (Courtesy KDKA.)

Bernie Armstrong (left) was musical director at KDKA Radio in the 1930s and 1940s. He led the staff orchestra and appeared on *Bernie Armstrong and His Men of Melody*. Bernie Armstrong at the organ provided the musical background for the *Dream Weaver*, a program of poetry by Marjorie Michaux read by Paul Shannon. Here Armstrong is shown with Buzz Aston (second from left) and Bill Hinds (far right) flanking an unidentified female vocalist. (Courtesy Judith Hinds Boehm.)

Thomas "Slim" Bryant and his Georgia Wildcats joined KDKA on August 10, 1940, at the invitation of program director George Hyde and in June 1941 became part of their new morning *Farm Hour*, performing between farm reports, sports, and news. They were also among the performers on the inaugural broadcast of Pittsburgh's first television station, WDTV, from the Syria Mosque. They recorded many songs for the NBC Thesaurus Transcription Library, which was distributed to hundreds of radio stations. Slim's photograph with a KDKA microphone is displayed in an exhibit in the Country Music Hall of Fame in Nashville. Pictured with Bryant are Wildcats Loppy Bryant (Slim's brother), Al Azzaro, and Ken Newton.

Shortly after his voice changed, Joe Negri gave up singing and began to seriously study the guitar. At age 16, he left Pittsburgh to tour with the Shep Fields Orchestra and then joined the army. In the late 1940s, Negri was back on Pittsburgh radio again, working at KDKA under musical director Bernie Armstrong. (Courtesy Joe Negri.)

In 1950, *Tommy Riggs and Betty Lou* was broadcast on CBS. Pittsburgher Tommy Riggs (and his Betty Lou voice) was first heard nationally on the *Rudy Vallee* show in 1937–1938. Quaker Oats then sponsored the first Tommy and Betty Lou series. His network radio career was interrupted when Riggs served in the navy in World War II. Tommy Riggs and Betty Lou received a star on the Hollywood Walk of Fame. (Courtesy Jim Riggs.)

Bette Smiley began as a disc jockey at KQV after high school, applying for the job on a dare. Her radio career lasted 20 years, during which she also appeared on Pittsburgh stations KDKA, KQV, WWSW, WCAE, and WTAE. Her *Radio Gift Shop of the Air* was syndicated on the Mutual Broadcasting Network and featured Bette interviewing popular entertainers, reading poetry, singing while playing piano live with a studio band, and reading letters from listeners. (Courtesy Rob Wesley.)

1080 On Your Dial **W P G H** PITTSBURGH, PA. **1000** WATTS

TWO SEA QUEENS DOCK SIDE-BY-SIDE
New York, still festooned with some of the snow remaining from the last blizzard, presents a fabely cold face to the Queens Elizabeth, left, and Mary as they docked side by side in the Hudson River. Actually Father Knick gave a warm welcome to these world's two largest liners arriving in the Yule season. It is the first time the two big liners have been in port here in peace-time service.

Everyone's favorite polkas
PENNSY POLKAS
By popular choice
1:00 p.m.   Monday through Friday

WPGH began broadcasting in 1947. Perry Marshall was one of the air personalities. He says that although most people assume that the station's call letters refer to Pittsburgh, they actually stand for Westview Park George Harton. George M. Harton II was the president of Westview Park, which Marshall recalls owned the station.

Joe Tucker was the voice of the Pittsburgh Steelers beginning with their first game broadcast in 1936 (from a Morse code transcriber) until 1967. He also announced play-by-play baseball, hockey, and golf, as well as a daily sports show from 1936 to 1968. Tucker (left) is shown with former heavyweight boxing champion Jack Dempsey (center) at a promotion at the Bonds Store for his nightly WWSW *Sport Special* show. The man at right is unidentified. (Courtesy Joe Tucker Archives/Murray Tucker.)

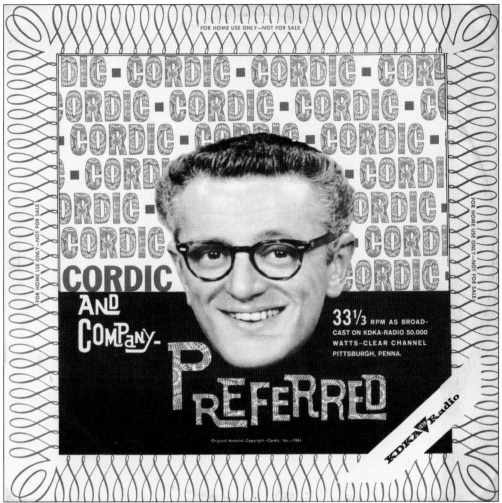

CORDIC AND COMPANY—PREFERRED

33⅓ RPM AS BROAD-CAST ON KDKA-RADIO 50,000 WATTS-CLEAR CHANNEL PITTSBURGH, PENNA.

Original Material Copyright—Cordic, Inc.—1961

KDKA 1020 Radio

Rege Cordic began his radio career at WWSW in 1934 and established his market-leading morning show in the 1940s when Davy Tyson left that station to join WCAE. On Labor Day 1954, Cordic moved his show to KDKA radio, replacing the *Ed and Rainbow* morning show. Cordic's "Company" included Bob Trow, Karl Hardman, Bob McCully, Charlie Sords, Sterling Yates, and engineer Bill Stefan. Characters included punster Carman Monoxide, philosophical Slav garbage man Louie Adamchevitz, tipsy golf pro Max Korfendigas, and Omicron, the bottle-shaped bureaucrat from Venus. His once mythical Olde Frothingslosh, "the Pale Stale Ale—so light the foam is on the bottom," was offered annually by the Pittsburgh Brewing Company.

Tommy Riggs's first radio job was at WCAE as half of the piano team of Riggs and Moake, but when the program director discovered Tom's Betty Lou voice, the *Tom and Betty Show* was born. Within a few short years, Riggs was doing the act on network radio. In 1955, he returned to WCAE as music director and afternoon disc jockey. (Courtesy Jim Riggs.)

Ira Apple, shown in 1955 in the control room of WEDO, McKeesport, excelled on both sides of the microphone. Ira did news and the *Austin Phone Party* on WAMP (WJAS) from 1959 to 1964. He then produced Mike Levine's talk show on KDKA and became executive producer and later program manager. He returned to WJAS in 1970 to do a talk show before becoming news director at KQV in 1973. (Courtesy Ira Apple.)

Nicknamed "The Gunner," Bob Prince is best known for his 28 years broadcasting the Pittsburgh Pirates games. In 1941, he became the host of *Case of Sports* on WJAS radio in Pittsburgh. Prince was an announcer for Pirates games from 1948 to 1975. He popularized pet phrases including "how sweet it is," "we had 'em all the way," and "kiss it good-bye!" He also created colorful nicknames for numerous Pirates players, such as "The Alhambra Kid" for Ralph Kiner, "Arriba" and "The Great One" for Roberto Clemente, and "Pops" and "Willie the Starge" for Willie Stargell. (Courtesy Joe Tucker Archives/Murray Tucker.)

"Uncle" Ed Schaughency joined KDKA as an actor in the *Kiddies Club* in 1932. In 1935, he began anchoring a morning program. In 1938, he was teamed with Elmer Waltman as the *Ed and Rainbow Show*. In 1954, Ed switched to afternoons and then to the news department, where he would spend the rest of his career, mostly as the morning newsman. Schaughency retired in 1980 after 48 years at KDKA. (Courtesy KDKA.)

Homestead's the Station of Nations, WHOD was founded in 1948 and aired programs including *Jewish Gems, Tony Ortale's Italian Hour, Chester's Polka Parade, Alex Avlon's Grecian Melodies,* and *Movin' Around with Mary Dee*. In 1956, new owners renamed the station WAMO, an acronym for the Allegheny, Monongahela, and Ohio Rivers. It became the first full-time country station in Pittsburgh with the *Porky Chedwick Show* the only exception.

W
ALLEGHENY
MONONGAHELA
OHIO

Pittsburgh's Country & Western Music Station

104 E. 7TH AVE., HOMESTEAD, PA., PITTSBURGH   HO 2-6000

Back row, left to right:

CARL STUART - MARTY KRAUS - SLIM BRYANT

Front row, left to right:

LOPPY BRYANT - ABBIE NEAL - PORKY CHEDWICK

860 ON YOUR DIAL

WEDO has kept the same call letters since signing on the air in 1947. During the 1950s, it carried a variety of network and locally originated programming. In the 1960s, WEDO became known for its Top 40 music presentation. In the 1970s, WEDO relocated its studios and offices inside Midtown Plaza Mall on Fifth Avenue in downtown McKeesport. Shoppers could watch the broadcasts. This matchbook is a 1950s promotional item.

"Your Pal" Pallan began his radio career at WWSW in 1942. Art Pallan joined KDKA in 1956 as they were making the switch from programs to disc jockey shows. In 1958, Art was the first to play "Since I Don't Have You" by Pittsburgh group the Skyliners. Art teamed up with Bob Trow for the morning show from 1965 to 1968 and stayed at KDKA until his retirement in 1985. (Courtesy KDKA.)

WJAS deejay Barry Kaye was one of the first in Pittsburgh to incorporate rock and roll into his program. Here Barry (left) is shown with 1950s hit maker Tony Bennett. Barry recorded the interracial rock and roll group, the Del Vikings, in his basement. He played their "Come Go with Me" on his show, which interested local label Fee Bee Records in making the proper studio recording, which became the hit. (Courtesy Barry Kaye.)

WJAS's Barry Kaye would take busloads of his listeners to New York for weekend trips to meet the stars. In Pittsburgh, he presented more stars at his record hops and rock and roll shows, like one at the Syria Mosque in May 1957 that featured Bo Diddley, the Clovers, and the Moonglows. That year, Barry was featured in the movie *Jamboree*, in which he was introduced by Dick Clark. (Courtesy Barry Kaye.)

In 1957, Jay Michael's afternoon show was part of a varied line-up on WCAE that featured Davey Tyson mornings, Tommy Riggs midday, and easy listening music overnights. His slogan was "relax with Jay everyday," but he was also one of the few to play rock and roll in the era before Top 40 radio, making him a favorite of teenage listeners. After leaving Pittsburgh, he worked in radio in California, ultimately playing pop music standards on stations in the San Diego area. (Courtesy Cynthia Mozingo.)

WCAE's Jay Michael is shown backstage at a concert with Nat King Cole, who became America's first black television star with the *Nat King Cole Show* in 1956. Jay was one of the first deejays to play records by black artists on mainstream radio and exposed local acts, including the El Venos, the Smoothtones, and the Orlandos (whose record was on the Cindy label, named for Jay's daughter). (Courtesy Cynthia Mozingo.)

Two

AM Radio Reinvents Itself

Radio reinvented itself when television became popular in the 1950s. Many of network radio's biggest stars, including Arthur Godfrey, Milton Berl, and George Burns and Gracie Allen, made the transition to television. Radio shifted from live musical programming, dramas, and quiz shows, now available on television, and began to rely primarily on phonograph records as their source of programming. At first, each radio station continued to offer "block programming," with each show different. In the early 1950s, station owners Todd Storz and Gordon McLendon found that the repetition of hit songs, programmed consistently throughout the day, was more successful than offering different programs. That "Top 40" approach was adopted by stations throughout the country. Storz veteran Ralph Beaudin was hired from KOWH in Omaha to be KQV's first general manager when the station changed format to Top 40. Rock and roll and rhythm and blues music were proving to be powerful programming for radio, especially in Pittsburgh.

Perry Marshall is shown at the console of WEEP. Perry had worked at the station when it was WPGH and left in 1954 when it became WILY. Perry recalls that he was the first deejay to broadcast the new format, making him Pittsburgh's first Top 40 deejay. When Neil Sedaka appeared at one of Marshall's record hops, Marshall, knowing that Sedaka was a classically trained pianist, asked him to play live. Concerned that the teenagers would not like classical music, Sedaka reluctantly agreed. Marshall reports he was a big hit. (Courtesy Perry Marshall; photograph by A. Church.)

KQV deejay Al Nobel attended the Skyliners' recording session for "Since I Don't Have You" on December 3, 1958, at Capitol Recording Studios at 151 West Forty-sixth Street in New York City. Pictured from left to right are Jack Taylor, Wally Lester, Nobel, Janet Vogel, Joe Versharen, and Jimmy Beaumont. (Courtesy John Taylor.)

"Chucky from Kentucky," Chuck Dougherty (left), hosted mornings and was program director at KQV in 1958 when the station switched to a Top 40 format. He stayed with KQV until 1960. In this photograph, he interviews Ward Darby, a local artist who had relocated from West Virginia. Darby had a few local hits, notably the instrumental "Safari," which reached No. 9 on KQV's chart in 1959. (Courtesy Ward Darby.)

The Best of Everything on *1320* Radio!

The Davey Tyson Show
6 A.M.-10 A.M.
Monday Through Saturday

Jane Ellen Ball
12:05 P. M.-12:30 P. M.
Monday Through Friday

Hilary Bogden
10 P. M.-2 A. M.
Gaslight Serenade

Beckley Smith News
12:30 P. M.-6:30 P. M.
Monday Through Friday

Ira Apple
Local News
On The Half-Hour

Bill Knupp
10 P. M.-2 A. M.
Gaslight Serenade

Bob James
Local News
On The Half-Hour

The Jim White Show
4 P. M.-7:30 P. M.
Monday Through Friday

Pittsburgh's Top Personalities...plus...

The Frank Tomasello Sho
12:35 P. M.-2 P. M.
12:05 P. M.-3 P. M. Sat.
Monday Through Friday

THE BEST FROM NBC RADIO!

NEWS
Pittsburgh's Best
Coverage!
NATIONAL NEWS
ON THE HOUR
LOCAL NEWS
ON THE HALF-HOUR
Plus
Direct Reports
From the
WAMP
Moibile News Unit

- NBC Radio News-On-The-Hour
- 10:05 A. M.—My True Story
- 11:05 A. M.—NBC Radio Theater

- 2:05 P. M.—It's Network Time
- 6:45 P. M.—Three Star Extra
- 7:30 P. M.—News of the World
  (with Morgan Beatty)
- 8:05 P. M.—Monitor

WAMP
NBC RADIO IN PITTSBURGH

WAMP, originally and later known as WJAS, signed on August 4, 1922, and was Pittsburgh's NBC affiliate in the late 1950s. Morning show host Davy Tyson worked 45 years in Pittsburgh-area radio, including WWSW and WCAE. Beckley Smith, a news broadcaster with an authoritative delivery, was heard for many years on both WJAS and KQV. Jim White was a deejay on WJAS but joined KDKA as a newsman. He later worked for 30 years at KMOX, St. Louis. June Ellen Ball was noted for her interviews with prominent Pittsburghers. Frank Tomasello later became a newsman at the station but also had a magic shop in the Fulton Building. Hillary Bogden had the advantage of being the only deejay playing rock and roll music in the late evening time slot. (Courtesy Ira Apple.)

WEEP SHEET

Pittsburgh's Top 40 Hits of the Week

TOP HITS OF PITTSBURGH, ACCORDING TO RECORD AND SHEET MUSIC SALES, JUKE BOX OPERATORS AND WEEP REQUESTS AS DETERMINED BY THE **CERTIFIED** WEEP SURVEY.

James P. Hensley
WEEP General Manager

WEEK ENDING September 27, 1958   Volume 1 Survey 49

PICK OF THE WEEP: Call Me - Johnny Mathis

TONY GRAHAM
8:45 A.M. to 11:45 A.M.

PERRY MARSHALL
1:45 P.M. to 5:45 P.M.

MERLE POLLIS
News Alive at 0:45
Every Hour

			Last Week
* 1.	It's All In The Game	Tommy Edwards	1
2.	Tea For Two Cha Cha	T. Dorsey Orchestra	2
3.	Nel Blu DiPinto Di Blu	Domenico Modugno	3
4.	Susie Darling	Robin Luke	4
5.	Bird Dog	Everly Brothers	5
6.	Devoted To You	Everly Brothers	--
7.	Tears On My Pillow	Imperials	6
8.	La Paloma	Bobby Day	7
9.	King Creole	Elvis Presley	12
*10.	The End	Earl Grant	15
11.	You Cheated	The Shields	10
*12.	Little Star	Elegants	9
13.	Stupid Cupid	Connie Francis	14
14.	Down The Aisle Of Love	The Quin-tones	25
15.	No One But You	The Ames Brothers	29
16.	Chantilly Lace	Big Bopper	21
17.	Just A Dream	Jimmy Clanton	11
18.	Week End	The Kingsmen	13
19.	I Wish	The Platters	36
20.	Put A Ring On My Finger	Les Paul & Mary Ford	24
21.	Patricia	Perez Prado	16
22.	Cerveza	Boots Brown	20
23.	Count Every Star	Rivieras	19
24.	Near You	Roger Williams	23
*25.	Promise Me, Love	Andy Williams	32
26.	You're Looking At Me	Johnny Nash	22
27.	Over The Week End	The Playboys	17
28.	No One Knows	Dion & The Belmonts	--
29.	Firefly	Tony Bennett	35
30.	Splish Splash	Bobby Darin	26
31.	Western Movies	The Olympics	18
*32.	A Promise Of Things To Come	David Hill & His Men	39
33.	Gee, But It's Lonely	Pat Boone	--
34.	The Day The Rains Came	Jane Morgan	--
35.	Fibbin'	Patti Page	--
36.	Are You Really Mine	Jimmie Rodgers	27
37.	Big Daddy	Jill Corey	--
*38.	Dance Everyone Dance	Betty Madigan	34
39.	Be Sure	The Dubs	31
*40.	Marianna	Lou Monte	--

* Former WEEP Pick of the WEEP

TOP TEN ALBUMS

1. King Creole .... Elvis Presley
2. Johnny's Great Hits .... Johnny Mathis
3. Swing Softly .... Johnny Mathis
4. Billy Vaughn Plays The Million Sellers .... Billy Vaughn
5. South Pacific .... Sound Track
6. Star Dust .... Pat Boone
7. The Best Of The Ames Brothers .... Ames Brothers
8. Elvis' Golden Records .... Elvis Presley
9. Sing Along With Mitch Miller...Mitch Miller & The Gang
10. Como's Golden Records .... Perry Como

RADIO 108...WEEP...*for* Joy!

LATIMER PRINTERS & LITHOGRAPHERS, INC.

In the fall of 1957, WILY changed call letters to WEEP and from a format serving specifically African Americans to Pittsburgh's first full-time Top 40 station. According to a *Time* magazine article, WILY was "possibly the loudest and zaniest radio station in the U.S." This 1958 WEEP playlist pictured deejays Tony Graham, Perry Marshall, and newsman Merle Pollis. The only WILY holdover, John "Sir Walter" Christian, had already left the station. (Courtesy Jay Brooks.)

Ed and Wendy King launched *Party Line*, considered the first radio talk show, on KDKA in January 1951. The callers' voices were never heard on the air, and there were no political or otherwise controversial discussions. There was a nightly "Party Pretzel" question and other games included Leapfrog, Alphabet Soup, Word Tag, and Digit. Listener letters were also read. The show aired until Ed King's death in 1971. (Courtesy Jack Bogut.)

Bill Steinbach began his 36-year career at KDKA in 1956 after graduating from Duquesne University. He was known as the Dean of Pittsburgh Radio Newscasters. He is best remembered as anchor of the station's *90 to Six* newscast, which began as a 30-minute newscast but grew to 90 minutes as it became more popular. (Courtesy KDKA.)

In October 1958, KQV moved its studios and master control from the 14th floor to the ground floor of the Chamber of Commerce Building at the corner of Stanwix Street and Forbes Avenue. Passersby could see the broadcasts from the "showcase studio windows." (Courtesy Carl Eckels.)

Terry Lee began his radio career in 1959 at WESA in Charleroi. He later worked at WZUM and WARO before winding up at WMCK/WIXZ. His record hops included TL's Nite Train just outside West Elizabeth and Redd's Beach in Fallowfield, the White Elephant, Burke Glen Ballroom, Red Rooster, and Varsity House and fire halls and social clubs throughout the Mon Valley.

THE FABULOUS 5 PLUS ONE

CHUCK DOUGHERTY

HENRY DaBECCO

ROY ELWELL

DAVE SCOTT

LEE VOGEL

JIM McLAUGHLIN

KQV's air staff in January 1959 included Chuck Dougherty, Henry DaBecco, Roy Elwell, Dave Scott, Lee Vogel, and Jim McLaughlin. The station also featured the *Breakfast Club* with Don McNeill at 9:00 a.m. and *KQV Newscope* at 6:30 p.m. KQV's news staff of Ken Hildebrand, Alan Boal, Jim Hunter, and Bob McKee delivered headlines at 25 minutes past the hour and a newscast at 55 minutes past the hour.

Porky Chedwick is widely considered to be the first disc jockey to make the trend of playing old records popular. He is also said to be the first Caucasian deejay in a major Eastern market to play black music for a racially diverse audience. Porky called himself "The Bossman," "The Platter Pushin' Poppa," and "The Daddy-o of the Radio" (with radio pronounced to rhyme with "daddy-o"). He called the songs he played his "dusty discs," since he would literally have to blow the dust from the forgotten 78-rpm records.

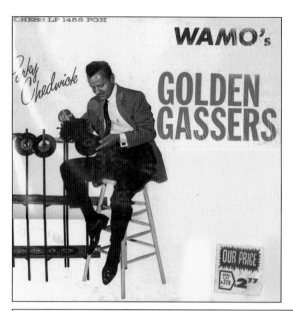

WAMO's *Golden Gassers* was the first of many Porky Chedwick oldies albums. The record contained songs that had become standards on his show. The same compilation was issued in other cities, with other station deejays pictured. After the success of this album in Pittsburgh, Porky would have quite a few similar albums distributed only in the Pittsburgh market.

LARRY AIKEN'S "Gold Dust"

POCO LOCO – Gene & Eunice

TONIGHT I FELL IN LOVE
The Tokens

SINCERELY – The Moonglows

CHURCH BELLS MAY RING
The Willows

I'LL BE HOME – The Flamingos

LONELY NIGHTS – The Hearts

HAPPY, HAPPY BIRTHDAY BABY
The Tune Weavers

ALONE – The Shepherd Sisters

A SUNDAY KIND OF LOVE
The Harptones

THIS SHOULD GO ON FOREVER
Rod Bernard

A THOUSAND STARS
The Rivileers

A KISS FROM YOUR LIPS
The Flamingos

KQV Radio

Larry Aiken's *Gold Dust* album featured oldies he played on his evening show at KQV and at his record hops. Larry joined KQV in 1959 and worked overnights, early and late evenings, and finally afternoons, at which time he was also music director. Larry left KQV in 1962 to open a concert promotion business in his hometown of Evansville, Indiana.

Clark Race joined KDKA in 1959 and at one point attracted 50 percent of the radio audience in his time slot. He was the major exponent of rock and roll on the station and would play a greater variety of music. Beatles manager Brian Epstein invited Race to go to London to meet the group. As the market leader, KDKA would have been the likely station to promote the Beatles' Pittsburgh concert except that KQV program director John Rook says that his friendship with Epstein's secretary resulted in Race being denied a promised seat on the plane with the Beatles on their flight to Pittsburgh, when he complained about Chuck Brinkman and Dex Allen being denied that same privilege. In 1969, Race left KDKA for the West Coast, where he worked at KMPC in Los Angeles and at stations in San Francisco and San Diego. He also hosted the ABC TV game show *The Parent Game*.

Rod Roddy became best known as the announcer for *The Price Is Right* from 1986 until the time of his death in 2003. Rod joined KQV April 25, 1960, for the evening shift from KOMA in Oklahoma City. In April 1961, Rod moved to KQV's morning show. Rod left KQV in June 1961. (Courtesy Georgia Radio Hall of Fame.)

WCAE newsman Keeve Berman (right) is shown in 1960 with comedian Soupy Sales. Berman worked at WCAE and WEDO before joining KQV from 1962 to 1967. After spending several years at WOR-FM in New York City, he briefly returned to Pittsburgh to work at WTAE in 1973 before returning to New York to work at the ABC Radio Network.

WAMO-FM was established in the early 1960s on 105.9. After a testing period, it instituted an all-jazz format as WAZZ. The on-air staff included Paul Blair, John Eastman, Zane Knauss, Tony Mowod, Glenn Tryon, and, briefly, John "Sir Walter" Christian. A couple years later, the station would revert to WAMO-FM and simulcast the AM format, promoting the combo as "the Double WAMO." (Courtesy Bobby Vinton.)

Bill Powell came to Pittsburgh from WSOK in Nashville, where he had hosted the *Bouncin' with Billy* show. He joined Lee "3-D Lee D" Doris at WILY, the area's first station targeted to black listeners. After that station changed to a Top 40 format as WEEP, Bill joined WAMO when it switched from a predominantly country format to rhythm and blues to capture WILY's former audience.

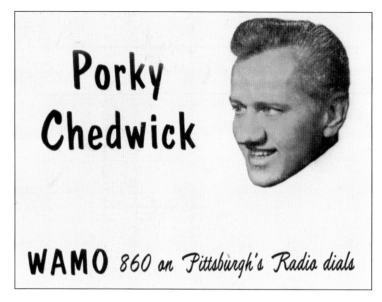

Porky Chedwick literally shut down the city with a remote broadcast he did at the Stanley Theater in downtown Pittsburgh during a showing of *Birdman of Alcatraz* in 1962. More than 10,000 listeners crowded the streets. Police estimated that there were another 50,000 in transit, causing such a traffic jam that Mayor Joseph M. Barr was reported to request that the broadcast cease.

WAMO is best known for consistent African American programming, which it adopted when WILY left that format in 1958. Pictured are, from left to right, "The Big Three" WAMO air personalities: Bill Powell, "Sir Walter" Raleigh (John Christian), and Chedwick. "Sir Walter" did mornings, Powell hosted middays, and Chedwick broadcast afternoons.

WAMO's Bill Powell presented Bobby Vinton with one of his first industry awards, Outstanding Big Band of 1960, at the Bill Powell Pittsburgher Awards, held at Carnegie Music Hall on April 21, 1961. Pictured from left to right are Harold Davis, president of Musicians Local No. 60; Bill Powell; and Vinton. Vinton was locally famous for his band before he ever had hit records as a vocalist. (Courtesy Bobby Vinton.)

KDKA's Clark Race (left) and Jim Williams (right) are seen with Bobby Vinton in the KDKA studios in the mid-1960s listening to Vinton's newest release. Vinton credits Race with breaking his first hit "Roses Are Red," which Vinton promoted himself by having roses delivered to local radio station deejays. (Courtesy Bobby Vinton.)

Jim Gearhart replaced Bill Western as KQV's morning personality in January 1962 and stayed for about two years. His A.S.E.N.I.N.E. organization (American Society to Eliminate Nudity in Insects) encouraged listeners to send clothing that was then displayed in KQV's Showcase Studio window. Gearhart left to become program director and morning host at WPOP, Hartford.

Randy Hall was the overnight air personality on KDKA in the early 1960s and was the original host of the *Saturday Dance Party* on KDKA-TV until Clark Race became host.

This KQV vehicle is the mobile studio used beginning in 1963 through the early 1970s. Promoted as a first for Pittsburgh, it was a rolling radio studio that was completely self-contained. This mobile unit claimed to be as fully equipped with modern technical equipment as any studio could contain, including a rest lounge and heating and cooling system. (Courtesy Jeff Roteman.)

KDKA radio's Clark Race has been called the "Dick Clark of Pittsburgh." His *Clark Race Dance Party* show on KDKA-TV, which featured local teens dancing to the current records, as well as live performances by recording artists, ran from 1963 to 1966. After a career in radio and television on the West Coast, Race retired from broadcasting and returned to the Pittsburgh area in 1986 to operate a bed-and-breakfast. (Courtesy Jack Bogut.)

The KQV Fun Lovin' Five, pictured in 1963, are Dave Scott (afternoons), Chuck Brinkman (evenings), Jolly Jim McLaughlin (overnights), Jim Gearhart (mornings), and Henry DaBecco (middays). Although it was a full-time Top 40 station, KQV also carried the ABC network's variety show Don McNeill's *Breakfast Club*, which originated in Chicago. The KQV news staff included Alton Crouch, Alan Boal, William Jennings, and Keeve Berman. Pie Traynor did sportscasts.

THE FIRST ANNUAL

WEEP CLUB
Custom Auto Show...

coming to
GREAT SOUTHERN SHOPPING CENTER
SATURDAY, APRIL 11, 1964

Grand Prize

to be awarded by a
majority of
WEEP CLUB Members Present

To enter, send a picture and a written
description of your car to "Auto Show"
WEEP, 210 Wood Street, Pittsburgh 22,
Penna. Sorry, no photographs can be
returned. Listen to WEEP for more
exciting details.

Cut here and send to WEEP

- - - - - - - - - - - - - - - -

APPLICATION FOR
WEEP CLUB MEMBERSHIP

Name_____

Address_____

Town_____

Phone_____Age_____

School_____

Main Interest_____

WEEP held a Custom Auto Show at the Great Southern Shopping Center on Saturday, April 11, 1964. Listeners were asked to send a photograph and description of their car, indicate their school, and apply for a membership in the WEEP Club. A grand prize was to be awarded by a majority vote of WEEP Club members present.

MURRAY THE MAGNIFICENT

HAL MURRAY • 6—10 A.M.
KQV — Audio 14

In 1964, "Emperor" Hal Murray's *Murray-Go-Round* show was brought to KQV by program director John Rook, who had worked with Murray in Denver. Pictured is the front of a Murray's Militia membership card numbered B 2540. Murray left KQV in 1967 but returned for a brief period in 1975.

KDKA's Clark Race was master of ceremonies for the Dave Clark Five's concert at the Civic Arena on June 5, 1964. Other acts on the bill included the Pixies Three, the Secrets, and Bobby Comstock and the Counts, who backed those two acts. Also appearing were Pittsburgh's own Fenways, whose "Humpty Dumpty" was a current local hit.

KQV presented the Rolling Stones in 1964 on their first U.S. tour before they had a hit record. This flyer promoted the event, which included two local acts: the Fenways and the El Rays. The crowd reacted to the then unknown group's long hair with catcalls and by throwing wads of paper at them.

You Are Invited To A

- *Blast* -

BOB MACK

❖ ❖ From Zoom Radio ❖ ❖

Operator Of These Dances:

White Elephant
Bethel Park Arena
Wildwood Lodge
Tarena

COMES TO

Teen Land !!

SATURDAY NIGHTS

MACKS' Sounds Will Blow Your Doors Off

Come On And Have Your Fun - Saturday

In 1962, Bob Mack began *Mack's Wax Museum* on WZUM radio, playing records that were popular in the teen dances he ran. The show lasted until 1964, when he resigned after station management insisted he include current rhythm and blues hits in his program. In addition to promoting his dances on his radio show, Mack distributed flyers like this in their immediate area.

KQV's Fun Lovin' Five presented their Summer Shower of Stars at the Syria Mosque on Monday, July 13, 1964. This was actually the Dick Clark Caravan of Stars tour, without Dick Clark, and included Gene Pitney, the Crystals, the Shirelles, the Reflections, the Dixie Cups, the Supremes, Major Lance, and others.

KQV's Fun Lovin' Five presented their Summer Shower of Stars No. 2 at the Syria Mosque for two shows on Saturday, August 1, 1964. This was actually the Show of Stars with the Four Seasons tour. The show also included Bobby Goldsboro, Ruby and the Romantics, the Chiffons, Barbara Lewis, Patty and the Emblems, and Jimmy Soul.

KQV's
"FUN LOVIN' FIVE"
PRESENT

The Four Seasons

Bobby Goldsboro   SUMMER   The Chiffons

SHOWER

OF

Ruby and the Romantics   STARS   Barbara Lewis

NO. 2

Patty and the Emblems   Jimmy Soul

PLUS . . .
KQV's Fun-Lovin Five
Hal Murray, Steve Rizen, Dave Scott
Chuck Brinkman, Dex Allen

TWO SHOWS - 7 P.M. and 9:30 P.M.

Saturday, August 1

Syria Mosque

tickets now on sale at all
NATIONAL RECORD MARTS

"Mad Mike" Metrovich was best known for his shows on WZUM beginning in August 1964. Mike introduced wild and obscure music to his radio listeners and to those who attended the many dances he deejayed, particularly at West View Park Danceland. Metrovich had previously been on WPIT and after leaving WZUM did shows on WYEP-FM, WEDO, and WWCS.

Steve Rizen

Dave Scott

Chuck Brinkman

Dex Allen

THE BEATLES

Hal Murray

kqv's Fun Lovin' Five welcome the Beatles to Pittsburgh, September 14.

In 1964, KDKA and KQV competed to be Pittsburgh's foremost Beatles station. KDKA had the advantage of exclusive interviews done by Group W correspondents who were traveling with the Beatles. KQV had a relationship with the local promoter, Tim Tormey, so it was KQV's Chuck Brinkman who had the honor of stepping up to the mike at the Civic Arena and announcing, "KQV welcomes the Beatles."

The KQV deejays (known as the Fun Lovin' Five), as pictured on the Finest Forty sheet at the height of Beatlemania, included Hal Murray (mornings), Steve Rizen (middays), Dave Scott (afternoons), Chuck Brinkman (evenings), and Dexter Allen (overnights). The station identified itself as "Audio 14 Pittsburgh" and used the slogan "The Summer Sound of Pittsburgh."

KQV scheduled news at 25 and 55 minutes past the hour so that they would be back playing music when most stations began their newscasts on the hour and half hour. In October 1964, the KQV news staff included Al Julius, Mark Schaefer, Keeve Berman, and Bill Jennings. KQV paid $25 for the best news tip each week.

Dave Scott worked at KQV from 1942 until 1968 and was the only member of the air staff retained when the station switched to Top 40. He briefly worked in Cleveland as a newsman but returned to Pittsburgh to work as a country deejay at WEEP.

KQV's Fun Lovin' Five (Hal Murray, Steve Rizen, Dave Scott, Chuck Brinkman, and Dex Allen) presented the Thanksgiving Shower of Stars for two shows at the Syria Mosque on Wednesday, November 25, 1964. Headlining the show was Chuck Berry, supported by the Supremes, the Drifters, Lou Christie, Brian Highland, the Crystals, and others.

KQV program director John Rook came up with this amphibious vehicle when KQV news was unable to give on-the-spot coverage of Pittsburgh's floods. He drove it to and from his home on the Monongahela River, attracting attention for KQV. When the novelty wore off, the station gave it away in a contest. When the winner drove off, the vehicle sank as the result of a plug inadvertently left open. (Courtesy John Rook.)

Bob Livorio was a WKPA, New Kensington, deejay remembered for his Saturday morning oldies show and his record hops. One night someone, either a college student home for vacation or Record City owner Ernie Kashauer, brought him a record on the obscure Snap label. Livorio played it at the dance and then on the radio. That record, "Hanky Panky" by Tommy James and the Shondells, soon became a national hit.

REGE CORDIC
6–10 AM

ART PALLAN
10 AM–2 PM

BOB TRACEY
2–4 PM

CLARK RACE
4–8 PM

KURT RUSSELL
Midnight–6 AM

KDKA RADIO 1020 GROUP W
SOUND ONE for MUSIC and FUN

In the 1960s, KDKA competed with KQV for the Pittsburgh contemporary music audience. Pictured, from top to bottom, is the deejay lineup from the back of KDKA's Sound Ones of 1964 sheet: Rege Cordic (mornings), Art Pallan (middays), Bob Tracey (afternoons), Clark Race (early evenings), and Kurt Russell (overnights). Not pictured are Ed and Wendy King, whose *Party Line* talk show ran evenings.

In April 1965, KQV held a contest on the back of their Finest Forty Survey in which listeners were asked to identify the baby pictures of the Fun Lovin' Five (Hal Murray, Steve Rizen, Dave Scott, Chuck Brinkman, and Dex Allen). The first 50 persons submitting the correct answers received their choice of five records from that week's list, which included songs by the Beatles, Elvis, and the Four Seasons.

kqv

AUDIO 14 PITTSBURGH

The Sound of Pittsburgh
KQV's Official "FINEST FORTY"

LAST WEEK	THIS WEEK	July 27-August 2, 1965
1	1	*UNCHAINED MELODY ... RIGHTEOUS BROS. - PHILLES
2	2	*WHAT'S NEW PUSSYCAT........Tom Jones - Parrot
5	3	*CALIFORNIA GIRLS............Beach Boys - Capitol
8	4	*SAVE YOUR HEART FOR ME......Gary Lewis - Liberty
4	5	*SATISFACTION ....Rolling Stones - London
3	6	*I'M HENRY THE 8th I AM ......Herman's Hermits - MGM
13	7	*I GOT YOU BABE ....Sonny & Cher - Atco
10	8	I LIKE IT LIKE THAT.........Dave Clark Five - Epic
9	9	*CARA MIA ....Jay & Americans - United Artist
6	10	*SEVENTH SON.............Johnny Rivers - Imperial
7	11	*WHAT THE WORLD NEEDS
		NOW IS LOVE ....Jackie DeShannon - Imperial
11	12	YES, I'M READY ....Barbara Mason - Arctic
12	13	YOU TURN ME ON ....Ian Whitcomb - Tower
18	14	*I WANT CANDY ....The Strangeloves - Bang
16	15	*Hold Me Thrill Me Kiss Me ......Mel Carter - Imperial
17	16	*All I Really Want To Do..........Cher - Imperial
24	17	*Down In The Boondocks......Billy Joe Royal - Columbia
26	18	Don't Just Stand There ....Patty Duke - United Artist
14	19	I Can't Help Myself............Four Tops - Motown
25	20	*Take Me Back ....Little Anthony - DCP
31	21	*Help ....The Beatles - Capitol
15	22	*Easy Question ....Elvis Presley - RCA Victor
32	23	*Happy Feet Time ....The Monclairs - Sunburst
23	24	*Theme From A Summer Place.....The Lettermen - Capitol
20	25	*Sunshine, Lollipops & Rainbows ...Lesley Gore - Mercury
22	26	*Here Comes The Night ....Them - Parrot
22	27	*Ride Your Pony ....Lee Dorsey - Amy
19	28	*Mr. Tambourine Man............The Byrds - Columbia
34	29	*Papa's Got A Brand New Bag ....James Brown - King
28	30	*Pretty Little Baby............Marvin Gaye - Motown
27	31	*A Little Bit of Heaven........Ronnie Dove - Diamond
35	32	*To Know You Is To Love You .....Peter & Gordon - Capitol
40	33	*Action ....Freddie Cannon - Warners
29	34	*Marie ....The Bachelors - London
--	35	*You'd Better Come Home ......Petula Clark - Warners
--	36	*It's The Same Old Song ....The Four Tops - Motown
37	37	Sitting In The Dark ....Billy Stewart - Chess
--	38	*Since I Lost You Baby.........The Temptations - Gordy
--	39	*Moonlight & Roses ....Vic Dana - Dolton
--	40	*Nothing But Heartaches ....The Supremes - Motown

* FIRST HEARD ON KQV

This survey is compiled each week by KQV Radio from reports of all record sales gathered from leading record outlets in the Pittsburgh area, requests, and from music information tabulated nationally.

A
U
D
I
O
14

KQV'S
FUN-LOVIN'
FIVE

Hal Murray   Steve Rizen
Dave Scott   Chuck Brinkman   Dexter Allen

A
U
D
I
O
14

WHO IS WHO?

...rectly identify each of KQV's **Fun Lovin Five** below by writing the correct name on the line below each photo. The first 50 correct entries will win any five of their favorite "Finest Forty" hits. Underline the five "finest forty" hits you would like to have on the reverse side of this sheet. Entries must be received at Station by April 6. Mail entire sheet to:

"FINEST FORTY SURVEY"
KQV Radio
Pittsburgh 19, Pa.

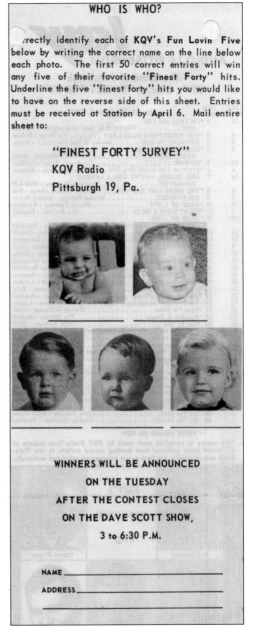

WINNERS WILL BE ANNOUNCED

ON THE TUESDAY

AFTER THE CONTEST CLOSES

ON THE DAVE SCOTT SHOW,

3 to 6:30 P.M.

NAME _____

ADDRESS _____

Big Steve Rizen switched shifts with Hal Murray, moving to the morning slot at KQV in July 1965. KQV program director John Rook brought Rizen to KQV from KTLK in Denver for middays in May 1964, replacing Henry DaBecco. Steve was 6 feet tall and weighed 265 pounds and said he was often mistaken for Hoss Cartright of the television show *Bonanza*, especially when he wore a Stetson hat.

KQV's Fun Lovin' Five meet one of the biggest hit makers of the rock-and-roll era, Connie Francis, when she visited the station in 1965. Pictured from left to right are Chuck Brinkman, Dex Allen, Steve Rizen, Francis, Dave Scott, and Hal Murray. Program director John Rook is in the background. (Courtesy John Rook.)

KQVips, as the deejays were known then, receive gold records for "Chapel of Love" and "People Say" by the Dixie Cups, "Remember (Walkin' in the Sand)" and "Leader of the Pack" by the Shangri-Las, and "I Wanna Love Him So Bad" by the Jelly Beans. Pictured from left to right are (first row) KQVips Hal Murray, Chuck Brinkman, and Dex Allen with Fenway Distributors' Jack Hakim; (second row) KQV program director John Rook, Fenway Distributors' Nick Cenci, KQVips Dave Scott and Steve Rizen, and Red Bird's George Goldner. (Courtesy John Rook.)

The Headliners was a local band that played at record hops held by deejays from KQV, WAMO, and WZUM, including Chuck Brinkman, Porky Chedwick, and Al Gee. All members attended South Hills Catholic High School. Pictured performing in 1965 are Mike Hickman (vocals), Dennis Auth (drums), Ed Salamon (guitar), and John Catizone (keyboards) at a record hop for KQV's overnight air personality Dex Allen, partially visible sitting behind the group.

KQV's Chuck Brinkman interviews Walter Shenson, producer of "A Hard Day's Night," while vacationing with the Beatles in the Bahamas in 1965. Brinkman and Dex Allen had met the Beatles in Baltimore the day before their Pittsburgh concert, and Brinkman introduced them at the Civic Arena. (Courtesy John Rook.)

WZUM ★

THE BEST in R & B in PITTSBURGH RADIO

1590 On Your Radio Dial • Offices and Studios 201 Ewing Rd., • P.O. Box 4442 • Pittsburgh, 5 Pa.

Phone 922-0550

THE SOUL SOUND

1590 TOP OF THE DIAL

Week of May 17th, 1966

TIGER ACTION SURVEY

AL GEE

ANDREA GRIFFIN

LORAN MANN

1. Cool Jerk . . . . The Capitols
2. It's A Man's World . . . . James Brown
3. When A Man Loves A Woman . . . . . Percy Sledge
4. Roadrunner . . . . Jr. Walker & The Allstars
5. Barefootin . . . . Robert Parker
6. Hold On I'm Comin . . . . Sam & Dave
7. Don't Waste Your Time . . . . The Five Stairsteps
8. Nothing's Too Good For My Baby . . Stevie Wonder
9. Love is Like An Itching In My Heart . The Supremes
10. Better Use Your Head . . . . Little Anthony & The Imperials
11. Greetings (This Is Uncle Sam) . . . . . The Monitors
12. S Y S L J F M (Letter Song) . . . . Joe Tex
13. You're The One . . . . The Marvellettes
14. Function At The Junction . . . . Shorty Long
15. Countdown . . . . Dave "Baby" Cortez
16. Just A Little Misunderstanding . . . . The Contours
17. Ain't Too Proud To Beg . . . . The Temptations
18. Wang Dang Doodle . . . . Koko Taylor
19. Take This Heart Of Mine . . . . Marvin Gaye
20. Take Some Time Out . . . . The Isley Brothers
21. All In My Mind . . . . Chuck Jackson
22. It's A Big Mistake . . . . The Royalettes
23. Loving You Is Sweeter Than Ever . The Four Tops
24. Good Time Charlie . . . . Bobby Bland
25. When A Woman Loves A Man . . . . . Ester Phillips
26. Ninety-Nine And A Half . . . . Wilson Picket
27. It's An Uphill Climb To The Bottom . . . . . Walter Jackson
28. Hot Shot . . . . The Buena Vistas
29. Don't Mess With Cupid . . . . Otis Redding
30. Hide Out . . . . The Hideaways

PLASTIC TO GOLD

Lover Boy . . . . The Blossoms

FEATURE ALBUMS:

Together . . . . Mary Wells & Marvin Gaye
A Touch Of Today . . . . Nancy Wilson

WZUM TIGER EXTRAS:

Chica Boo . . . . Googie Rene Combo
That's Life . . . . O. C. Smith
He's Ready . . . . The Poppies
Please Baby Please . . . . The Sensations

And More - - -

BOUNCIN BOBBY BENNETT

JEFFREY TROY

MAD MIKE

WZUM had adopted a rhythm and blues format by mid-1966. The air staff included Al Gee, Andrea Griffin, Loran Mann, Bouncin' Bobby Bennett, Jeffrey Troy, and Mad Mike Metrovich. Al Gee went on to work at other stations, including WWRL, WLIB, and WPIX (all in New York City) and hosted the nationally syndicated *Rap N' Rhythm* show. Loran Mann left for KDKA and had a 30-year career in broadcasting. Bobby Bennett left for WAMO and worked at WOL, WTOP, and WHUR in Washington, D.C. Jeffrey Troy worked at WWRL in New York City. Mad Mike deviated from the regular station format, playing his signature Mad Mike Moldies.

When Rege Cordic decided to go to Los Angeles in 1965, KDKA kept Bob Trow, who had done voices on the show, to continue some of the characters from *Cordic and Company*. A Westinghouse executive in New York suggested that he be teamed with Art Pallan, and *Pallan and Trow . . . Two for the Show* debuted on Monday, November 29, 1965.

The KQV deejays (still known as the Fun Lovin' Five, as pictured on the Finest Forty sheet during the Summer of Love) included Bob Wilson (mornings), Jonny Mitchell (middays), Dave Scott (afternoons), Chuck Brinkman (evenings), and Tom Lee (overnights). Mitchell would soon leave, and Scott and Brinkman would move one shift earlier to make room for Jim Quinn.

Jim Horne was hired for overnights at KDKA by program director Tony Graham in 1967. He was promoted to evenings and then afternoons, where he worked until 1972. He also did a short-lived Saturday evening talk show. Jim then worked for former KDKA program director Neil McIntyre at WPIX-FM in New York before launching an acting career on Broadway, as well as in television, movies, and commercials as J. R. Horne.

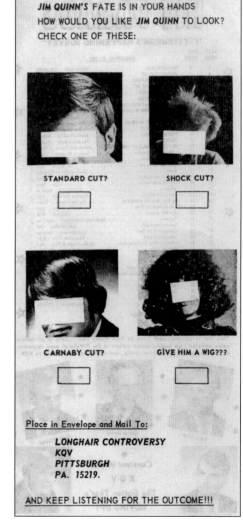

Long hair was still controversial in January 1968, and KQV's evening air personality Jim Quinn had longer hair than anyone else on the air staff. Listeners were asked to vote whether Jim should keep his "Carnaby Cut" or adopt a shorter "Standard Cut." According to his photographs on later KQV Hit Parade sheets, Jim kept his haircut for a while longer.

Rex Miller joined KQV for mornings in February 1968, was moved to overnights, and left the station in April. He worked at some of the biggest Top 40 stations in America, including KLIF, Dallas; WPRO, Providence; WQXI, Atlanta; and WITH, Baltimore, where this photograph was taken several years before he moved to KQV. After leaving radio, Rex was the author of several horror novels. (Courtesy John Long.)

KQV's Truck O' Luck was the vehicle used in 1968 in a company-wide promotion done by the ABC Top 40 stations promising "door to door delivery of prizes." KQV and sister stations WABC in New York and WLS in Chicago put the Truck O' Luck on the streets loaded with prizes. In Chicago, WLS called it the Treasure Truck. (Courtesy Jeff Roteman.)

Myron Cope joined WTAE in 1968 as a sports commentator, despite having a nasal voice and pronounced Pittsburgh accent, both of which were quite a departure from the radio announcers of the time. In 1971, he began 30 years of color commentary for the Pittsburgh Steelers games. He is perhaps best remembered for his "Copeisms" ("yoi," "Okel dokel," and "mmm-haa") and as one of the creators of the Terrible Towel in 1975. In 2005, Cope became the first pro football announcer to be inducted into the National Radio Hall of Fame. (Courtesy WTAE.)

Todd Chase replaced Jim Quinn on KQV's evening shift in July 1968. Later that year, he moved into the noon–3:00 p.m. time slot. Todd left Pittsburgh to work at radio stations in Miami but returned as program director of 96.1 WHTX in 1986. After a successful career in secular radio, Todd began working on the air at a Christian radio station in Florida.

LISTEN FOR THE "Double Golden"

Featured on the all NEW
Todd Chase SHOW

PEPSI-COLA Pours It On!

The KQV Radio 14 deejays as pictured on the Hit Parade, Pittsburgh's Happening Survey, in the fall of 1968 included Franklin B. Forbes (overnights), Allan Dennis (middays), Bob Wilson (mornings), Chuck Brinkman (afternoon drive), Todd Chase (evenings), and Johnny Mitchell (early afternoon). On January 1, KQV had dropped ABC's Don McNeill's *Breakfast Club*, one of the last of the daily network entertainment programs.

Franklin B. Forbes   Allan Dennis   Bob Wilson

Chuck Brinkman   Todd Chase   Johnny Mitchell

FRED WINSTON 10 A.M. – 2 P.M.

Fred Winston joined KQV in 1968, where he would do both mornings and midday. He also voiced many of the KQV IDs during his tenure. Winston had worked at KOIL in Omaha, WING in Dayton, and WKYC in Cleveland. In 1971, former KQV program director John Rook brought him to WLS in Chicago, and he remained in that city, working a number of stations for more than three decades. (Courtesy Bob Wood.)

In January 1969, Harry West was hired from WARM in Scranton by program director Mike McCormack to host the *Harry West Show* mornings on KQV. Harry remained in that position until December 1971, when he returned to northeastern Pennsylvania for the remainder of his career. (Courtesy Bob Wood.)

HARRY WEST 6 A.M. – 10 A.M.

Jack Bogut, one of radio's great storytellers, replaced Pallan and Trow mornings on KDKA in 1968. *Bogut's Mental Movies*, extemporaneous stories told over a music background, are considered among the best examples of radio as theater of the mind. Both ABC's *Good Morning America* and *USA TODAY* featured Jack as one of the top five morning show personalities in the nation. He left KDKA to join WTAE. Bogut was later recruited to WSSH and then moved to sister station WJAS. Here Bogut is shown on a billboard from the early 1970s with the rainbow used in "KDKA's Pittsburgh: Some Place Special" campaign. (Courtesy Jack Bogut.)

In 1969, the Westchester Corporation purchased McKeesport's WMCK and changed its call letters to WIXZ. Patterned after their successful Cleveland Top 40 station, WIXY, WIXZ tried to compete with KQV, despite KQV's better signal and coverage of the market. That rivalry is depicted by the billboards in the photograph. WIXZ then moved to a rock and gold format and then to country before switching to talk as WPTT and later WMNY.

KQV's Jim Quinn is shown here on a motorcycle, one of the "loves of his life" according to a feature on the deejay in the November 1969 edition of *TV Radio Mirror*. The article further says that "sometimes as a change of pace, he straps some clothes onto his motorbike and goes a travelin'—sans maps and direction—just takes off!" (Courtesy Carl Eckels.)

Terry Lee was the only air talent held over when the Westchester Corporation purchased WMCK. T. L. was known for his program of obscure records, known as *Pittsburgh Oldies,* and especially for his *Music for Young Lovers* segment, which featured romantic ballads. At this time, Terry Lee was also hosting Channel 11's teen dance show, *Come Alive.*

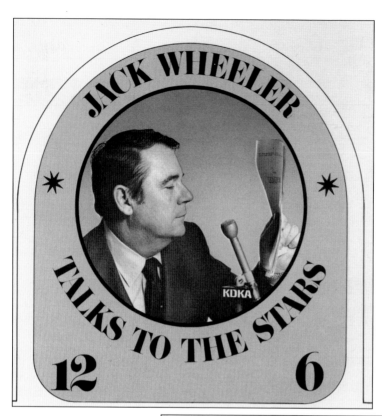

Jack Wheeler joined KDKA in the summer of 1969, replacing the all-night music show with talk. He also hosted a KDKA-TV show, *Some of My Best Friends*, utilizing many of the celebrities who appeared on his radio show. In 1974, Jack left to do the morning show at WEEP. His controversial approach to talk, combined with country music, helped to give that station its largest listening audience.

Mike Levine was a former newspaper reporter who became a radio newsman and talk show host of *Contact* and *Open Mike*. Levine joined KDKA in 1958 and left to work at sister station WINS in New York in 1968, returning in 1970. In 1975, Levine joined WEEP during its short period as a talk station and then spent a couple years at a Miami station before rejoining KDKA.

On November 2, 1970, the U.S. Postal Service honored KDKA with a special cancellation stating "50th Anniversary of Broadcasting 2 November," marking the Harding-Cox election broadcast. Congressman James G. Fulton arranged for the postmark, which served as an official U.S. government sanction of KDKA's claim as the first radio station.

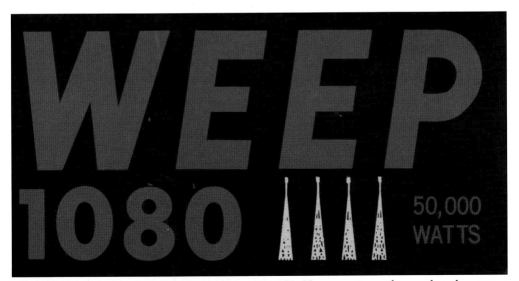

WEEP began broadcasting with 50,000 watts in 1970. However, it was licensed at that power for only a few hours each day. WEEP was a daytime station, with sign-on and sign-off times that changed each month. WEEP's format through the 1970s was country, except for a brief period of talk in the middle of that decade.

Perry Marshall returned to WJAS in 1970 after a four-year absence and was soon hosting the evening show Sunday through Friday on the station, which was by then talk. A station brochure described Perry as "a credit to those who assert that radio is still a quality medium." He remained with the station until it switched formats to Top 40 as 13-Q. (Courtesy Perry Marshall.)

WJAS was the first radio station in the world to make use of the Bell Telephone Picturephone when it put the device in operation during a remote broadcast at Gimbels Department Store on July 1, 1970. At the time, there were about 100 subscribers to the service, mostly businesses. Pictured is Ira Apple (left) talking to fellow WJAS talk show host Joe Gearing during a test run. (Courtesy Ira Apple.)

WJAS adopted a talk format in the late 1960s, becoming Pittsburgh's first all-talk radio station. The talent lineup, known as the "Communicasters," included, from left to right above, Joe Gearing, Bill Ross, Perry Marshall, Ted Payne, and Ira Apple. Ira had done the first talk show broadcast on that station when it was known as WAMP. The air staff met weekly to exchange suggestions and to be briefed on upcoming guests and new WJAS features. (Courtesy Ira Apple.)

WIXZ program director Chuck Dunaway was interviewed by KDKA-TV's Stuart Brown prior to a meeting with Pittsburgh mayor Pete Flaherty regarding the cancellation of the station's permit to hold a concert in Schenley Park. City officials were concerned because of riots at rock concerts in other cities. Iron Butterfly had been booked to headline the event, which would have attracted an estimated 40,000 WIXZ listeners. (Courtesy Chuck Dunaway.)

Sean Grabowski was the name WIXZ midday host, whose real name was Bill Rock, was asked to use in 1970, hoping to get attention from Pittsburgh's large Irish and Polish population. He was the focus of promotions, including a cow-milking contest and having listeners count the leaves in tea bags. Bill later became a fixture in New York radio and television and now owns his own award-winning production company. (Courtesy Bill Rock.)

Three

THE GROWTH OF FM RADIO

The FCC mandated separation of AM and FM programming as of January 1, 1967. On that date, FM stations in markets with populations over 100,000 were prohibited from simulcasting more that 50 percent of the programming of their AM parent. That encouraged owners to create different programming for their FM stations. In those early years, FM radio was a place for experimentation and an opportunity for young people interested in radio who could accept the low salaries this new medium could afford. Coincidentally, at this same time, artists began to release songs that AM stations thought were too controversial or too long. FM radio attracted a young audience by embracing this music in underground and progressive rock formats. Although FM provided competition to the already entrenched stations on the AM band, FM listenership remained small until the early 1970s, when GM, Ford, and Chrysler made AM-FM radios standard. For nearly a decade, AM radio held on to the majority of radio listeners. Advertisers became more sophisticated and stations' audiences became more targeted as the number of stations grew. Radio personalities switched from AM to FM and vice versa as station formats changed. It was not until 1978 that FM listenership exceeded AM listenership for the first time.

Kenny Reeth came to Pittsburgh in 1962 to sign on a new station, WZUM, where he was known as Skinny Kenny. He was part of the nightclub comedy team Reeth and King that hosted a morning radio show on WDRC in Hartford. He was hired at WAMO and later as vice president of programming for its owner, Dynamic Broadcasting. He left Pittsburgh in 1973 for Miami and then bought KKAR, a country station in Pomona, California. (Courtesy Frank Gottlieb.)

WAMO-FM listeners would not have guessed that this straitlaced-looking guy was Frank the Freak. This photograph was taken while Frank Gottlieb was doing the overnight shift on WAMO-FM before the station adopted an underground format. Frank says he and the studio looked the same during WAMO-FM's underground era. The difference was that he would be playing LPs rather than 45s and not using the cart machines for jingles. (Courtesy Frank Gottlieb.)

Brother Love's Underground was hosted by Kenny Reeth as Brother Love beginning in early 1968 on WAMO-FM. His sidekicks were Raymond the Condemned (Ray Anderson) and the Observer, who would communicate only by nonverbal means, like by clanging cymbals. This show introduced Pittsburghers to Jimi Hendrix, the Doors, Mothers of Invention, and other artists who became mainstays of Album Rock radio.

KDKA has helped raise funds for Children's Hospital by broadcasting from department store windows and malls during the Christmas season. The tradition of storefront broadcasts only began in the late 1960s. Pictured are Art Pallan and fans outside of Kaufmann's. (Courtesy KDKA.)

Bob Harper, KQV's program director from 1970 to 1973, transitioned the station from a teen to an adult Top 40 format, partially to avoid competition with sister station WDVE, whose Rock 'N' Stereo format (used by ABC's FM stations) he helped to create. He hired Jeff Christie, now better known as Rush Limbaugh. Harper added "New Golds," songs no longer current but not yet oldies, now known as "recurrents." (Courtesy Carl Eckels.)

Porky Chedwick is pictured on the phone at WAMO in the 1960s. When WAMO's program director, Ken Reeth, began playing underground rock music on WAMO-FM, he convinced Porky to do the same. Chedwick had a brief stint as "The Electric Ched Head." Porky soon returned to playing the "Dusty Discs," for which he is best known. (Courtesy Ed Weigle.)

KQV-FM separated from a simulcast of KQV in 1969 to run the love format, hosted 24 hours a day by Brother John Rydgren, which was syndicated to all seven of the FM stations owned by the ABC Network. The station went live in 1970 and in 1971 changed call letters to WDVE, for dove—the bird representing peace. It used a racetrack graphic as its logo, as did its sister stations.

Carl Eckels joined KQV as news director in 1971 and moved to sister station WDVE in the same capacity in 1974, remaining there until 1979. Carl remembers being attracted to a woman who passed the studio windows each day. One day, he persuaded fellow newsman Dave James to ask her a question and tell her she won a free lunch with the news director (Carl) because of her response. (Courtesy Carl Eckels.)

Jon Summers was at KQV from 1970 through 1973. During that time, he was the official master of ceremonies for all the concerts presented by Pat DeCaesar. Jon recalls having dinner with David Bowie, who was dressed in a suit made from Holiday Inn towels; having hot chocolate with the Osmonds; and getting to know Jim Croce, who played Pittsburgh a number of times. (Courtesy Carl Eckels.)

The Beaver Valley's Jaggerz visited KQV in 1970 to promote their soon-to-be No. 1 hit and million-selling single, "The Rapper." Shown from left to right are Jaggerz Donnie Iris, Bill Maybray, Tom Davies, and Jimmie Ross, KQV program director Mike McCormick, Benny Faiella, Jim Pugliano, and KQV music director and air personality Chuck Brinkman. (Courtesy Jimmie Ross.)

Terry Caywood is pictured at WZUM in the early 1970s when station owner Jimmy Pol and his dog, Polka Pete, hosted a morning polka show, while the rest of the day was progressive rock. In addition to Caywood, the rock air staff included Kit Baron, Michael Jon, and Paul Perry (the son of Pittsburgh television staple Nick Perry). (Courtesy Terry Caywood.)

The original WDVE air staff included Ted Ferguson (nights, far left), Dwight Douglas (production director, second from left), Carolyn Smith (mornings, third from left), Jessie (afternoons, top of tree), Don Davis (evenings, sitting), and Buddy Rich (middays, hanging upside down). (Courtesy Jessie Scott.)

Jessie became Pittsburgh's first female rock jock when she joined WDVE in 1971. After working at WYDD, she became one of the first women on a major market Top 40 station when she joined 13-Q in 1974. In 1975, she became the only female jock on the AM dial in New York when she joined country station WHN. She was the first female program director at XM Radio. (Courtesy Jessie Scott.)

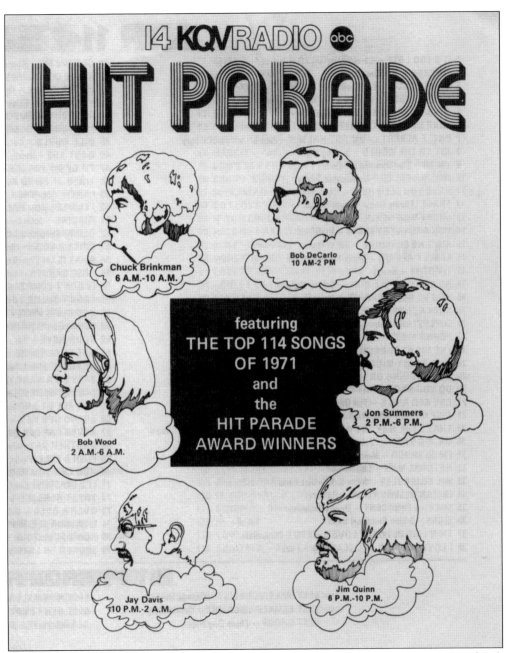

The KQVIPs—Chuck Brinkman, Bob DeCarlo, Jon Summers, Jim Quinn, Jay Davis, and Bob Wood—are pictured in Peter Max–style caricatures on this year-end hit list from 1971. KQV's daytime programming was aimed at adults, while evenings and nights still attracted teens. Jay Davis, also known as "Jay the Jock," had worked at WLOA, Braddock; WHJB, Greensburg; and WPSL, Monroeville. He would later work at WYDD and WDVE before leaving the air and becoming sales manager of WTAE and WHTX.

Bob Wood, "Woodburger," was the overnight deejay at KQV from 1970 to 1972. Bob recalls that he was offered the job as program director for KQV-FM when it was switching from an automated to live format. Since FM was not yet popular, he turned it down. Bob considers that decision a big mistake because the station eventually became the No. 1 station in Pittsburgh as WDVE. (Courtesy Bob Wood.)

WDVE hired so many Point Park College graduates that the college gave the station an award. Pictured are (seated) Kenny Lee (Spector) and Dwight Douglas; (standing, from left to right) WDVE staffers Paul Randall, Point Park professor Vince LaBarbara, Judd Levinson, general manager Steve Berger, Tom Daniels, Ron Chavis, and Bill Bruun. (Courtesy Dwight Douglas.)

Jack Bogut broadcasts from the Kaufmann's Department Store window while listeners line up outside to make donations to Children's Hospital of Pittsburgh in exchange for coffee and farkleberry tarts. In 1971, Bogut turned a fictional bush called the farkleberry into a major component of the annual fund-raising campaign and one of Pittsburgh's holiday season traditions. KDKA raised millions for Children's Hospital. (Courtesy Jack Bogut; photograph by Dick Brehl.)

Larry O'Brien joined WTAE for mornings in 1972 from legendary Top 40 station WCFL, Chicago, where he had been the evening personality. In April 1975, general manager Ted "Captain Showbiz" Atkins and program director Mark Roberts teamed Larry with afternoon personality John Garry for the morning show, resulting in one of Pittsburgh radio's most successful partnerships. (Courtesy Mark Roberts.)

John Garry joined WTAE for afternoons in 1972 from WGH, Norfolk, where he and future cohost Larry O'Brien had once worked at the same time. O'Brien and Garry invented characters including Lieutenant Macho and Mr. Science. They moved to WTAE's sister station, 96KX, as well as WMXP and WSSZ in Greensburg, before returning to WTAE. (Courtesy Mark Roberts.)

KDKA Radio's Rainbow Machine was the station's remote broadcast vehicle in the 1970s and early 1980s. This GMC motor home was a portable radio station that was used in broadcasts at sporting events, holiday parades, and so forth in and around the Pittsburgh area. The vehicle took its name from the logo of the "Pittsburgh: Some Place Special" campaign. (Courtesy KDKA.)

WIXZ bettered the traditional bumper sticker with their "sticky fingers" campaign. These die-cut fingers portrayed the peace sign depicted in campy retro artwork. Listeners were asked to display the stickers on the rear of their car. If their license number was announced on the air, participants could win prizes ranging from a Magnavox home entertainment center to albums. Many stickers were defaced to depict only the middle finger raised.

RAP-AROUND

with

Dennis Benson
Sundays 9:00 - 11:00 p.m.

KQV RADIO 14

*It's your chance to sound off,
ask questions, and seek advice.*

Dennis Benson, an ordained Presbyterian minister, hosted KQV's weekly Sunday evening *Rap-Around* in the early 1970s. He was one of the few religious leaders able to combine theology with the emerging rock music culture, thereby relating to youth. Benson would later host and produce the nationally syndicated public service radio series *Passages*.

The KQV Double Dribblers played basketball at schools and at fund-raisers for community organizations. All the players wore the station's dial position, 14. News director Carl Eckels was the coach and offered snappy patter during team introductions. Among those pictured are George Gilbert (sales), John Wagg (a ringer, who played at North Carolina), Chuck Brinkman, Jay Davis, Bob Harper (program director), Derek Hill (newsman), and Bob Wood. (Courtesy Carl Eckels.)

This was the KQV news vehicle in the early 1970s. At the time, television stations could not quickly send film crews on location, so radio was the primary source for on-the-spot coverage of breaking news stories in the Pittsburgh area. On August 1, 1972, Bob DeCarlo broadcast from the KQV mobile news car with newsman Bob Harvey helping motorists find parking spaces on the first day of the city's parking lot attendants strike. (Courtesy Carl Eckels.)

Joel Zelle replaced Jim Horne in afternoons at KDKA in 1972. He also did the Sunday morning show, where he played theme sets (records related by subject). The Sunday morning show had traditionally been a time period when KDKA broke format and played a broader range of music not usually heard on the station. Zelle is shown here at a bike promotion. (Courtesy Warren Maurer.)

KQV morning personality Bob DeCarlo was honorary ringmaster of the Ringling Brothers, Barnum and Bailey Circus matinee on November 3, 1973. DeCarlo suited up in ringmaster attire to ride an elephant promoting the station's involvement. (Courtesy Bob DeCarlo.)

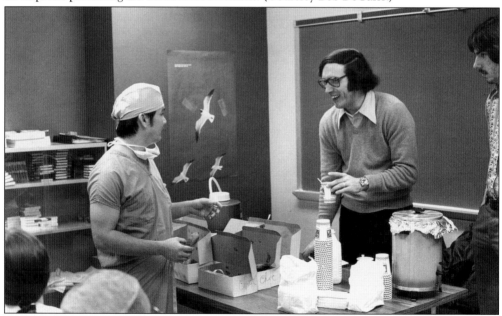

KQV's morning personality Bob DeCarlo personally delivered coffee and doughnuts to businesses listening to his show as an ongoing weekly promotion with the George S. Aiken Company. Bob is shown providing a coffee break to Dr. Virachal Theerakulstit and his staff at Shadyside Hospital, the business being saluted in the second week of January 1974. (Courtesy Bob DeCarlo.)

KDKA talk show host Mike Levine broadcasts from the backseat of a vehicle during the March of Dimes walk-a-thon in the early 1970s. Pittsburgh radio stations were very responsive to their community and gave airtime and sent their air personalities to promote charity events that may not have been successful without their promotion. (Courtesy Warren Maurer.)

KDKA's overnight personality, Jack Wheeler, interviews a participant in the March of Dimes walk-a-thon. The very first March of Dimes walk-a-thon occurred in San Antonio on October 7, 1970. The concept soon swept the nation. By 1974, a full 95 percent of March of Dimes chapters participated in the event, raising $14 million for the cause. (Courtesy Warren Maurer.)

WIXZ morning deejay Mike McGann introduces Cuba Gooding Sr. and the Main Ingredient at the VIP Club on the north side in October 1972. Gooding had taken over as the group's lead singer earlier that year and led their first major pop hit "Everybody Plays the Fool," which sold over one million copies. (Courtesy Mike McGann.)

Pittsburgh Pirate Al Oliver (left) chats with WIXZ morning deejay Mike McGann at one of the first radiothons for St. Jude Children's Research Hospital in October 1972. McGann had replaced Jeff Christie at WIXZ. At the time, the Pirates had just lost the playoffs to the Cincinnati Reds in the fifth game of the series because of a wild pitch. (Courtesy Mike McGann.)

BLOND WONDER WITH THE **RECORD THUNDER** PORKY CHEDWICK

Porky Chedwick joined KQV to do a weekend program in 1972. He left WAMO, where he had started in radio in 1948 when the station flipped to a contemporary urban format. Chedwick later rejoined 860 AM and resumed his *Dusty Disc* show when the station switched call letters to WYJZ and its primary format to jazz.

Sam Holman worked at KQV in 1958, but he is best remembered in Pittsburgh as one of the original 13-Q personalities. Sam took a brief hiatus from 13-Q's morning show but returned in April 1974. Sam was already an industry legend as a WABC, New York City, deejay and its first Top 40 program director and is considered one of the pioneers of Top 40 radio.

Cecil Heftel bought WJAS from NBC and debuted 13-Q on March 12, 1973, with a high-energy Top 40 format and a cash call contest where listeners could win $13,000 by answering their phones "I listen to the new sound of 13-Q" instead of "hello." That amount was a huge prize in the days before state lotteries, and many Pittsburghers, who would have never otherwise listened to the station, participated. At one point, the station was second only to KDKA in the ratings. At the end of that year, the staff included, from left to right, (first row) Mike Dineen, Batt Johnson, and program director Dave Daniels; (second row) Dennis Waters, Eddie Rogers, and Jack Armstrong; (third row) Earl Lewis and Dave Brooks. Not shown is Buzz Bennett, the consultant who conceptualized the station.

Jack Armstrong was one of the original 13-Q deejays; he stayed at the station for two years and then spent a short time at KDKA. When he arrived in Pittsburgh, he was already a legend from his work in Cleveland, Boston, and Buffalo. Armstrong was known for his fast talking and for his Gorilla character. In 1978, Jack was morning air personality at 10-Q, Los Angeles, the biggest market he ever worked.

KDKA's Art Pallan presents contest winners with airline tickets for a trip to a football game. Warren Maurer, then KDKA's general sales manager, recalls this as one of many promotions where listeners were asked to register at the location of an advertiser. The entries would then be put into a drum, visible in the background, and the winner drawn by station personnel. (Courtesy Warren Maurer.)

Thousands of Chances to Win!

LISTEN TO 14K MUSICRADIO FOR DETAILS

4K, we're making it easy for you to win in
Great 14K Giveaway:
eel off the large 14K Sticker (marked
nd put it on your car bumper
r your license plate. This
tles you to special
ounts on 14K-Day.

2. Peel off the smaller square 14K Sticker (mark
B) and put it on your home telepho
3. Peel off the other squa
coupon sticker (marked
stick it on a card a
carry it with y

KQV began calling itself 14K after the debut of Top 40 rival 13-Q in March 1973. Perry Marshall, then on middays at KQV, recalls that he had suggested the tag as a joke at a staff meeting when they were discussing 13-Q. The station returned to using KQV as their primary identifier in July 1974. (Courtesy Ira Apple.)

KDKA's John Cigna (center left) helps celebrate the grand opening of a new Hills Department Store in the North Hills. Cigna had recently joined the station as the 9:00 p.m.–midnight talk show host, replacing Ed and Wendy King's *Party Line*. (Courtesy Warren Maurer.)

Tom Martin was a newsman at KQV in 1973 and 1974, appearing with Bob DeCarlo on the morning show. He later joined the ABC Radio Network, where he was the vacation substitute host for the legendary Paul Harvey. (Courtesy Carl Eckels.)

Bob Pittman was the first program director of WPEZ, Pittsburgh's first FM Top 40 station. As Robert W. Pittman, he was later a founder of MTV and then became chief operating officer of AOL Time Warner, the world's largest media conglomerate. He is pictured with deejays Jim Davis and Buzz Brindle on the first WPEZ hit list, dated February 8, 1974. (Courtesy Ronald "Buzz" Brindle.)

Pittsburgh was one of the first markets in which radio stations telephoned listeners to ask them about their music preferences. Call-out research became common practice at 13-Q, WPEZ, WEEP, and other stations. The first local call-out music research was done at KDKA in 1970. Pictured is Ed Salamon speaking about call-out research at the Country Radio Seminar in Nashville in 1974.

"Little" Jimmy Roach is shown in the WDVE studios in the 1970s. Jimmy arrived from WCOL, Columbus, in 1973 and did the afternoon show until teaming up with Steve Hansen for the *DVE Morning Alternative* in 1980. Roach is credited with breaking Pittsburgher Donnie Iris's hit "Ah Leah" when he played it as an album track. (Courtesy Jimmy Roach.)

WEEP's Gary Semro was named the nation's leading major market country radio personality for 1974 by *Billboard* magazine. Gary came to WEEP from legendary Top 40 stations KHOW and KIMN in Denver, Colorado. Disgruntled that WEEP would not give him a raise, one day Gary quit on the air at the end of his show. He later worked as Gary Clark on WCBS-FM in New York and for the Jones Radio Network.

KQV's Jon Summers (left) and Larry Clark (right) are shown together in 1973. In 1975, Larry joined WEEP, replacing another former KQV alumnus, Timothy G. Adams, who had been recruited by a Chicago station. Although KQV was an adult-oriented Top 40 station and WEEP played country music, the stations had a similar on-air presentation, so it was an easy transition for these KQV personalities to make. (Courtesy Carl Eckels.)

John Cigna came to Pittsburgh as morning news anchor and sports director of WJAS. He joined KDKA as evening talk show host in 1973 and moved to mornings as part of the K-Team in 1983. Cigna is recognized for his longevity in the market, at KDKA and as a morning drive personality. He had a motorcycle accident in 1999 and retired from his top-rated morning show in 2001. (Courtesy KDKA.)

Buzz Brindle was one of the original deejays at WPEZ. He later worked at their AM rival, 13-Q, and also at KDKA before leaving for WNBC in New York. He then became director of music programming at MTV. Before Pittsburgh, he worked at stations in Providence, Washington, D.C., and Chicago. (Courtesy Ronald "Buzz" Brindle.)

Jack Armstrong married Miss Peggy in June 1974, and the 13-Q air staff attended the ceremony. Shown are Dennis Waters (middays), Jessie (early mornings), Batt Johnson (nights), Sam Holman (mornings), and Jack Armstrong (evenings). (Courtesy Jessie Scott.)

Dennis, Jessie, Batt, Sam, Jack
ROCK THE BOAT
INSTANT REQUEST LINE
333-9122

wtae BIG 300

Thanksgiving 1974

WTAE counted down Pittsburgh's favorite 300 songs on Thanksgiving weekend 1974. The air staff, as pictured on the cover of the list, was Larry O'Brien, Bill Hillgrove, John Garry, Mike McGann, Tom Lyons, Mark Roberts, and Chuck Brinkman. Bill Hillgrove had worked at WKJF. He went on to be the play-by-play announcer for the Pittsburgh Steelers and the Pitt Panthers. WIXZ veteran McGann later worked at 96X (WHKX) and WJAS. Like Chuck Brinkman, Tom Lyons had been heard on KQV, where he was known as Tom Lee. Roberts joined WTAE from WIXZ after having worked at their sister station WIXY in Cleveland.

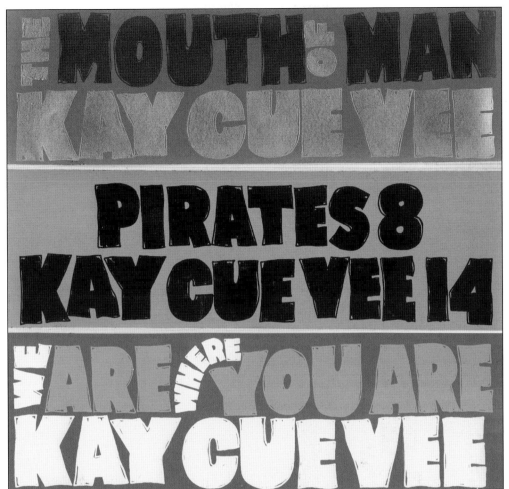

When KQV was sold by ABC to Taft Broadcasting, new general manager Bill Irwin hired legendary radio disc jockey Joey Reynolds as KQV's program director. Reynolds's air staff did not have predictable schedules; news was broadcast at various times ("because news doesn't happen on schedule"). When a record made it to the top of the KQV chart, it was dropped to avoid it being overplayed. Instead of a single slogan for the station, he had many. Pictured are some examples. Reynolds left the station in May. During his career, he worked at over two dozen legendary radio stations.

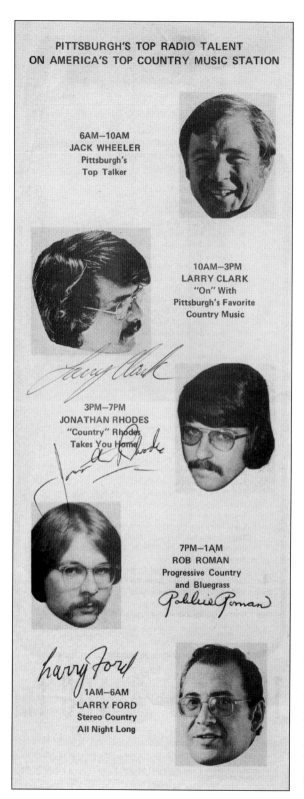

**PITTSBURGH'S TOP RADIO TALENT
ON AMERICA'S TOP COUNTRY MUSIC STATION**

6AM—10AM
JACK WHEELER
Pittsburgh's
Top Talker

10AM—3PM
LARRY CLARK
"On" With
Pittsburgh's Favorite
Country Music

3PM—7PM
JONATHAN RHODES
"Country" Rhodes
Takes You Home

7PM—1AM
ROB ROMAN
Progressive Country
and Bluegrass

1AM—6AM
LARRY FORD
Stereo Country
All Night Long

WEEP's lineup in May 1975 included Jack Wheeler (from KDKA), Larry Clark (from KQV), Jonathan Rhodes (from WSLR, Akron), Robbie Roman (who had been Wheeler's producer), and Larry Ford. At the time, WEEP had a larger audience share than any country station in a top-10 market. The following month, program director Ed Salamon was hired for the same position at WHN.

Steve Hansen is shown here when he did the evening show at WDVE in 1975. Steve left Pittsburgh for San Francisco for a couple of years, but he returned to be teamed with Jimmy Roach for mornings as the *DVE Morning Alternative*, and it became one of Pittsburgh's most successful radio shows. (Courtesy Terry Caywood.)

Robbie Roman hosted an evening country rock show on WEEP-FM in the mid-1970s, an attempt to reach the youthful audience on FM with a style of music compatible with the country music on the more popular WEEP-AM. Artists featured included the Eagles, Creedence Clearwater Revival, Marshall Tucker Band, and Pure Prairie League, mixed with roots country artists like Merle Haggard and George Jones.

WANTED

YOU---

IF YOU'RE INTO: THE EAGLES, WAYLON JENNINGS, MARSHALL-TUCKER BAND, NEW RIDERS, POCO, BLUE GRASS MUSIC, ETC.

ROBBIE ROMAN
STEREO 108 — 7PM-1AM
STARTS MARCH 31ST ON WEEP

KDKA's Jack Bogut faced off against Mayor Pete Flaherty at a Pittsburgh Penguins game. The winner did the other man's job for a day; the loser filled in to give the winner a day off and bought him lunch. Bogut won and was mayor of Pittsburgh on February 25, 1975. Flaherty did Bogut's show and must have liked it because in March he joined DeCarlo and Company's morning show on KQV. (Courtesy Jack Bogut.)

George Hart (left), shown with KQV music director Gary Waight, was teamed with Joe Fenn by program director Joey Reynolds, first as Frick and Frack then as Coal and Steel. Hart and Billy Soule played the last record on KQV October 14, 1975, *Brother Love's Travelling Salvation Show* by Neil Diamond. The station then switched to a news format. Hart went on to join 96KX as Sean McCoy. (Courtesy Terry Caywood.)

Pittsburgh Steelers quarterback Terry Bradshaw joined Bill Tanner on the 13-Q morning show during the 1975 football season. Arguably, this experience helped prepare Bradshaw for his later broadcast career. When Bradshaw retired from football in 1983, he signed a television contract with CBS to become an NFL game analyst. Prior to his full-time work for them, he served as a guest commentator for *CBS Sports*.

"Gather Sunshine Around You With CLAIROL SUNSHINE HARVEST SHAMPOO"

Vitas Gerulaitis led the Pittsburgh Triangles to the World Team Tennis Championship in 1975, at which time he was a WPEZ fan. He is pictured in a WPEZ Stereo Z T-shirt with afternoon deejay Buzz Brindle at a live station event that year. Gerulaitis is best known for winning the men's singles title at the Australian Open in 1977. (Courtesy Ronald "Buzz" Brindle.)

Don Cox was the quintessential rock-and-roll format disc jockey and worked at some of America's greatest Top 40 radio stations. He came to 13-Q in 1975 from Miami and left the station in 1977 for Los Angeles before spending the rest of his career in Miami. He was known for his bawdy on-air personality and double entendres.

In 1976, the Armored Q would award prizes to drivers with 13-Q bumper stickers on their cars. Pictured in front of the station vehicle are 13-Q deejays Buzz Brindle (left) and Dennis "The Menace" Waters, who also was program director at the time. Dennis later was on the air at WNBC in New York. (Courtesy Ronald "Buzz" Brindle.)

In May 1976, 13-Q ran a contest in which the winner got to meet the star of the hit television show *Welcome Back Kotter*. At that time, John Travolta was better known as Vinnie Barbarino, the character he played in that show, than by his own name. Buzz Brindle had moved from WPEZ to the midday slot on 13-Q. (Courtesy Ronald "Buzz" Brindle.)

Members of the KQV and WDVE air staff are shown picketing the stations during a 1976 strike called by their union, the American Federation of Radio and Television Artists. WDVE's Terry Caywood recalls that fellow deejay Marsy played Bob Dylan's record *Maggie's Farm* and left the studio. Program director John McGhan and other non-union employees filled in on the air until an agreement was reached. (Courtesy Carl Eckels.)

KDKA's Dave James broadcasts from a cow chip chucking festival. Jack Bogut makes the toss as professional golfer Ben Crenshaw prepares to try to hit a golf ball across the Allegheny River to Three Rivers Stadium. Bogut recalled that when one of the chips curled into the crowd, striking a spectator, James said, "Wow, the chip hit the fan." The comment was not only broadcast over the public address system but also live on KDKA radio. (Courtesy Jack Bogut.)

Jack Bogut participated in innumerable community activities during his years in Pittsburgh radio. A masterful speaker, here he entertains the Pittsburgh Chamber of Commerce. On the dais are, from left to right, Bishop Vincent Leonard, KDKA sportscaster Bob Prince, Allegheny County commissioner Tom Foerster, and Pittsburgh Steelers owner Art Rooney Sr. (Courtesy Jack Bogut.)

Jay Stevens was the air name of WEEP program director Joel Raab. He is shown in 1979 with country artist Bobby Bare, who visited the station, probably as a guest deejay. Rather than interview artists, WEEP would let them take over a radio show for an hour and read weather, traffic reports, and commercials and play music. (Courtesy Joel Raab.)

WDVE arranged for contest winners to meet and have their photograph taken with Kiss when the group performed at the Civic Arena on January 14, 1978, during the Alive II tour. Gene Simmons's "Demon" makeup reflected cynicism and a dark element. Paul Stanley's "Starchild" depicted him as "starry-eyed lover." Ace Frehley was a "Spaceman," and Peter Criss chose "Catman" believing he had had nine lives. WDVE's program director John McGhan is to Stanley's right. (Courtesy WDVE.)